A SURVEY OF THE IRISH IN ENGLAND (1872)

A SURVEY OF THE IRISH IN ENGLAND (1872)

HUGH HEINRICK

EDITED BY

ALAN O'DAY

THE HAMBLEDON PRESS

LONDON AND RONCEVERTE

Published by The Hambledon Press, 1990

102 Gloucester Avenue, London NW1 8HX (U.K.)

309 Greenbrier Avenue, Ronceverte WV 24970 (U.S.A.)

ISBN 1 85285 010 8

British Library Cataloguing in Progress Data

A Survey of the Irish in England (1872).
1. England. Irish immigrants. Social
conditions, 1872
I. O'Day, Alan
305.8'9162'042

Library of Congress Cataloging-in-Publication Data

Heinrick, Hugh, ca. 1830-1877.
A survey of the Irish in England (1872)
/Hugh Heinrick; edited by Alan O'Day.
Originally published in sixteen articles
in the Nation, a Dublin nationalist weekly
newspaper, between Jul6 6 and Nov. 9, 1872.
Includes bibliographical references.
1. Irish – English – History – 19th century –
Sources. 2. England – Ethnic relations – Sources.
I. O'Day, Alan. II. Title
DA125.17H45 1990 942'. 0049162 – dc20
89-48059 CIP

Printed and bound on acid-free paper in Great Britain
by Antony Rowe Ltd., Chippenham

Contents

To Geneviève Schauinger and
Christoph Mühlberg

Preface

Discovery of the extended series of newspaper articles titled, "The Irish in England" resulted from research undertaken for a chapter in Volume IV, "Political Representation", of the project, "Governments and Non-Dominant Ethnic Groups in Europe, 1850-1940" sponsored by the European Science Foundation. That series, largely ignored since publication in 1872, is of such interest that I am pleased to have an opportunity to make it widely accessible. Surprisingly little systematic information has been collected about the experience of Britain's most numerous immigrants and publication of the survey now is a small step towards filling the void. Perhaps it is best treated as a progress report on the exiles a little more than twenty years after fleeing Ireland and just prior to revival of massive migration at the close of the 1870s. Interest in the Irish has been rising, partly as a means for better understanding the Anglo-Irish relationship, to extend an appreciation of domestic social, religious and political development, and, to broaden knowledge of the process of immigration for an age coming to grips with the reality of the post-1945 influx of "strangers". Britain's membership in the European Economic Community with its free mobility of people across national boundaries, makes fuller historical investigation of immigrant communities imperative.

During preparation of this edition I have incurred many debts – foremost to the European Science Foundation, especially Christoph Mühlberg and Geneviève Schauinger in Strasbourg and my colleagues working under the guidance of Kevin B. Nowlan in Group IV of the project. I also received support and insights from members of Groups IV and VII. My research was supported by grants from the European Science Foundation, British Academy, Marc Fitch Fund, the Twenty-Seven Foundation and The Polytechnic of North London. Other participants in the project, especially Sheridan Gilley, Colin Pooley, Ellen Wiegandt and Donal Kerr have contributed important insights. Vital assistance has been provided by Roland Quinault, Michael Hurst, Geoffrey Crossick, John Hutchinson, David Fitzpatrick, Iain McLean, Paul Laxton and Roger Swift. Papers based on the edition were presented to sessions of Group IV, at the Metropolitan Seminar, Institute of Historical Research; the modern British History Seminar, University of Cambridge; and most completely at the Irish Studies/ Demography Seminar, University of Liverpool. As a consequence of suggestions offered on the last occasion, I revised the introduction.

I must pay special tribute to my mother and to my aunt, Colonel Helen O'Day, who over many years have offered generous moral and financial suport, which can never be repaid properly.

Alan O'Day
February 1989

Introduction

In July 1872 *The Nation*, a prominent nationalist weekly newspaper began a series of articles under the title "The Irish in England". That survey was initiated on 6 July and concluded on 9 November after running to sixteen parts spread over seventeen issues – one letter being of such length as to require publication in successive instalments. The series was published on consecutive weeks until 19 October. After a three week interval the final article appeared on 9 November. In total the survey was approximately 50,000 words long and the work of a single person, Hugh Heinrick, though the pieces were published under the by-line, "Our Special Commissioner" without reference to the author's identity. Heinrick's investigation was, as he claimed, the first comprehensive examination of the Irish community in England. The only later detailed investigation of the Irish in England prior to J.A. Jackson's, *The Irish in Britain*, published in 1963, was John Denvir's identically titled volume of 1892 (a second edition was released in 1894). Scotland's Irish community, not treated in the Heinrick articles, was the subject of two significant volumes by J.E. Handley both published in the 1940s.[1] Whereas the Denvir tome has remained a standard work of reference on the Irish community, the Heinrick survey has been almost completely overlooked. Denvir did not refer to it and Jackson appears to have been unaware of the Heinrick articles. With the exception of three unpublished theses, the series in *The Nation* has escaped notice.[2]

Relatively little is known about the author. Although he possessed an unusual surname, there is no account of its origin and Heinrick himself was evidently thoroughly Irish. Heinrick was born in county Wexford in the early 1830s.[3] After a period as a teacher in a national school he migrated to Birmingham. By the late 1860s Heinrick had resided in his adoptive city for many years. In Birmingham he was a teacher in Catholic schools and also a journalist. At the beginning of the 1870s he seems to have followed the latter occupation exclusively. Heinrick was a minor though active figure in local affairs, especially on behalf of Catholic and Irish interests. In 1871 he had himself described as having been for the previous five years one of the principal writers of *The Nation*.[4] His claim was probably an exaggeration for Heinrick did not live in Ireland then and the journal carried only a limited diet of news about England or its Irish community. Heinrick undoubtedly enlarged on his tie with *The Nation* in order to promote his role as proprietor of the *Irish Vindicator* which commenced publication on 30 September 1871. The weekly newspaper was published in London and aimed at the Irish there and elsewhere in England. In September Heinrick moved to the metropolis to run his enterprise. At the time no other periodical was aimed specifically at the immigrants. The journal concentrated almost entirely on affairs in Ireland, particularly emphasizing the growing home rule movement, and contained little information about the Irish in Britain. Much of the content was derivative, drawing especially heavily on *The Nation* and other Irish periodicals. His venture was not a success and the newspaper ceased operations after the issue of 9 December. Heinrick then returned to Birmingham.

The Nation had been established in 1842 and during its early era was a vehicle of the Young Ireland movement. For some years the newspaper was a beacon for literary and nationalist writers and, as a consequence, retained a certain lustre and reputation long after the collapse of Young Ireland. In the 1850s it came under the control of A.M. Sullivan, a man of considerable taste, and he was still the proprietor in the early 1870s. Sullivan was a constitutional nationalist and a devout Catholic. His journal reflected both outlooks. Sullivan was no friend of the Irish Republican Brotherhood. He, however, was a stanch ally of Cardinal Paul Cullen, the much admired or disliked, depending on the perspective, Archbishop of Dublin. Sullivan was anathema to Fenians. In the late 1860s and 70s *The Nation* was suspect to radical nationalists but still the most reliable and influential advocate of Irish aspirations. In the late 1860s the newspaper gave ardent support to the amensty campaign for release of the Fenian prisoners. With the foundation of the Home Government Association in 1870, *The Nation* became the foremost newspaper advocating home rule principles. Sullivan, and also his brothers, were prominent participants in the Dublin-based Home Goverment Association. In 1872 A.M. Sullivan was a member of the governing Council and attended Association meetings frequently. Both he and *The Nation* took a benevolent interest in the Irish in England. Increasingly after 1870 *The Nation* acted as a surrogate newspaper for the immigrants.

Motivation for the series of articles is explicable, in part, by the developing consciousness of the Irish in Britain. James Stephens, the Fenian Chief, was to assert that 80,000 Irishmen on the mainland belonged to his organization, and, in 1865 the British Government was convinced that some 18,000 actually did.[5] That number represented a potentially unsettling force in the event of a serious disturbance in Ireland. In 1867 just such a revolt did take place in the sister island: in England three spectacular incidents – the abortive raid on Chester Castle in February, the rescue of the Fenian prisoners in September at Manchester and the explosion outside the Clerkenwell House of Detention in December – set off waves of anti-Irish feeling in the host community. In June Birmingham experienced attacks on Irish Catholics.[6] Following the accidental death of Sergeant Brett in the Manchester rescue, *The Nation* commented, "we are only concerned for the hundreds of thousands of our people, who, after years of toil in the service of England, are threatened with extermination because the Government is baffled in pursuit of two brave and daring conspirators".[7] It thought, "the present panic will not be altogether regretted, if it convince our people of the stern necessity of closing their ranks in the face of the peril which menace them". Execution of the three men convicted of murdering Brett sparked off huge funeral processions in Manchester and London for the "martyrs" showing an intense level of national feeling among the exiles. In June 1868 *The Nation* exclaimed, "nowhere in England can our countrymen consider themselves safe from English mob violence . . .'[8] The newspaper recognized that the community necessarily stood in the front line of a hostile reaction to Irish national aspirations and proposed a National Relief and Defence Fund to assist them for:

> we do not seem to be entering upon a period of tranquillity. The Irish race at home and abroad are committed to a struggle for their political rights, and are determined to go on with it. That means a struggle against English injustice, English prejudice, and English class interests.

The Nation admitted that "it means risk and trouble and suffering, especially for the Irish people located in England".

The Reform Act of 1867 and the general election in 1868 gave the Irish added significance. Many now found themselves possessed of the ballot and, therefore, potentially able to exert an Irish influence in urban parliamentary contests. Gladstone's campaign on Irish issues in 1868 offered suggestive possibilities. For a start it placed Ireland firmly at the top of the political agenda. The triumph demonstrated that a unity of Irish and British Liberal electors on the mainland with Catholics in the Emerald Isle was very potent. Moreover, Gladstone's "mission to pacify Ireland" had been shaped particularly by the Clerkenwell outrage. Britain's Irish, it seemed, had exceptional powers of persuasion.

Between 1868 and 1870 the demand for clemency or amnesty of the Fenian political prisoners gained momentum. Demonstrations in Ireland and Britain to support the prisoners drew massive crowds. Amnesty was a truly "national" cause which enlisted men from all classes, religious professions and across party demarcations. As early as May 1867, Cullen, an uncompromising opponent of Fenianism, gave public support to the movement for clemency.[9] Issac Butt's forthright leadership of the campaign magnified his popularity. In 1869 the Liverpool Irish Liberal Association "originated from the difficulty experienced some time ago in getting up a public meeting for the release of the political prisoners, thereby showing the necessity of such an organisation of Irishmen, when any great question affecting their interests turned up".[10] Similarly, amnesty played a considerable part in bringing together people elsewhere interested in reform which in one instance culminated in mid-1870 in the foundation of the Birmingham Irish and English Association. The organizers declared, "as it owes its origin to a series of meetings held at the public offices to discuss the Irish question, its first attention will be directed to matters affecting the political and social state of Ireland . . ."[11] If the amnesty movement elevated Butt into a national spokesmen, it also marked Hugh Heinrick's low key advance in Irish affairs. Reports in *The Nation* from March 1868 reveal him as an activist in the prisoners interest. By the time of the Birmingham meeting in 1870 he was sufficiently prominent to be designated honorary secretary of the new association.

Above all the amnesty campaign fanned the desire for unity among Irishmen. It demonstrated that action across religious and class boundaries was possible. Moreover, this spirit received a fillip in the early months of 1870 as widespread dismay greeted Gladstone's Irish Land Bill. To many people it seemed that British Government, even when headed by Gladstone, would only be attentive to Irish opinion when unity in Ireland was achieved. In May the dual motives of a desire for co-operation and sense of illusionment brought forty-nine mainly Protestant gentlemen together at the Bilton Hotel in Dublin for the purpose of considering their country's future. In an editorial titled "The National Movement", *The Nation*, observed, "the assembly consisted almost entirely of gentlemen of high social and mercantile position who have hitherto been, we might say, unheard of in Irish politics".[12] It applauded "the glorious spirit of 1782 . . . manifest again in the speeches delivered by Irish Protestant gentlemen on the occasion". A decision was reached at the Bilton Hotel meeting, which was attended by Sullivan, to support Isaac Butt's federal home rule scheme. The new movement quickly roused impressive enthusiasm. An editorial in *The Nation* pointed out, "we are happy to inform our readers that the National Organisation inaugurated by a number of

Protestant gentlemen in Dublin, but which includes within its ranks men of all creeds and classes, progresses in a most hopeful and satisfactory manner".[13] In a long letter in July Hugh Heinrick defined the appeal of the movement during a discussion of the merits of federalism and repeal, explaining:

> I have myself joined the Committee of the Home Rule Association because I recognise in it a principle of union which, in all our political history, has never been before presented to us. Let us not mar this great principle by minor issues. Let the broad Bill of Home Rule be accepted. The details can be adjusted in Committee.[14]

Shortly thereafter *The Nation*, which had expressed reservations about Butt's scheme, echoed Heinrick's message when it argued that the precise meaning of federalism was "no great matter at the present stage. The one important and indispensable thing is that the popular intellect should get hold of the project generally, and try it by the unfailing test of examination and discussion."[15] Immediately afterwards the variegated complexion of the movement was revealed when the Home Government Association's first monthly meeting reported that its Committee contained several clergymen, a majority of Catholics and a Liberal proportion of three to two.[16]

During the second half of 1870 Home Rule advanced rapidly. An Irish meeting at Middlesbrough endorsed the proposal.[17] A number of groups in Ireland did likewise. Butt ably expressed Home Rule's appeal. In December he articulated effectively the mounting support for the plan, gave ventilation to an emergent self-conscious Irish feeling, and signalled the worldwide nature of the coming struggle when he insisted:

> they were not to crouch and whine at the feet of Engand, but to demand by moral force, their rights, and moral force was always strong when physical force was behind it. That physical force consisted in the existence of twelve millions of Irishmen scattered over the globe, whom England might unite in friendly federation, or whom she might make her foes.[18]

Butt's rhetoric fell on attentive ears. His plea that Ireland was to demand not beg struck deep into the Irish psyche.

Emphasis on the global character of Irish support was a comparative new aspect of Irish strategy. It resulted from the massive emigration of the Irish since the mid-1840s. Even prior to the Great Famine there was very extensive Irish emigration but the catastrophe of the '40s unleashed a flood of mainly impoverished unskilled hordes fleeing from their native land.[19] Britain was second only to the United States as the reception centre. In 1841 the decennial census enumerated Irish-born residents in England and Wales as 289,404, with a further 126,321 in Scotland. Ten years later the totals had leaped respectively to 519,959 and 207,367. In England and Wales the peak was reached in 1861 when 601,634 were recorded. In Scotland that census enumerated the numbers as 204,083. By 1871 the Irish-born had drifted downward to 566,540 in England but rose in Scotland to 207,770 not halting a climb until after 1881 when the total was 218,745. There were, then, a lot of Irish-born present in the early 1870s though even in 1861 in England and Wales they were only 3 per cent of the total population and in Scotland at the highest point in 1851, 7.16 per cent. Census enumerators only noted the place of birth thereby omitting British-born children. Even inclusion of all of this obviously important element did not lift the ethnic proportion above approximately 6 per cent of the whole population. Irish impact therefore was necessarily selective. Influence was confined to places where the concentration was substantial. London had the highest numbers but the Irish-born percentage even in 1851 was only 4.6 and in merely three registrar general's districts – St. Giles in the Fields, St. Olave, Southwark, and Whitchapel – did the numbers exceed a tenth of the population.[20] In the northern industrial cities there were more. Liverpool's Irish-born in 1851 constituted 22.29 per cent falling to 18.91 in 1861 and to 15.56 in 1871. For Manchester the comparable percentages for the same years were 13.08, 11.31 and 8.59 while in Glasgow they were 18.17, 15.70 and 14.32. In the important port city of Bristol in 1851 the Irish totalled under 3.5 per cent of the population.[21] A tiny number of smaller, mainly

Lancashire towns, like Wigan, had slightly higher percentages but the Irish did not constitute a majority in any British city of note.

Within areas of settlement the Irish tended to be clustered in certain districts. Heavy concentration presaged an effect in parliamentary elections and more certainly in municipal contests. That was implicit in the emphasis which Butt and other Irish figures accorded to the emigrés. Even in the most Irish of areas the picture was complex. Sophisticated analysis of Liverpool, the most Irish of the major cities in England, illustrates the difficulties of moulding the immigrants into a cohesive community.[22] By 1851 they already had settled in distinct pockets within the city. One of the three wards with more than 40 per cent Irish-born was in the south; the other two being in the north. By 1871 the respective enclaves were well-established and maintained largely separate existences. By then there were seven registrar general's enumeration districts with an Irish-born population in excess of 50 per cent and only one with none at all. By the 1870s dispersal and other factors militated against effective collective action throughout Liverpool. Even within each Irish cluster there was a marked residential predisposition based on county of origin in Ireland. Differences in Ireland were replicated thereby in Liverpool. As people advanced up the social ladder, they tended to drift to the geographical fringe of the residential concentration. In 1870 the northern enclaves were still relatively cohesive but that in the south, with its more mixed ethnic and social composition, left the Irish prone to other influences. Moreover, as residential choice was related in a significant way to occupation, questions of horizonal economic rivalry added to tensions within the Liverpool Irish community.

In a much less Irish city like Bristol the difficulties of establishing an ethnic communal life were magnified. As in other places, the Famine refugees showed a tendency to concentrate in certain types of mainly unskilled employment and were over-represented in some residential neighbourhoods. But even in 1851 Bristol did not have a "single well-defined Irish ghetto . . ."[23] They revealed a propensity for intermarriage with the host community – a trend most evident "in parishes where the Irish were less concentrated in particular streets or courts".[24] Isaac Butt's appeal to the Irish outside Ireland was both interesting and important but it was one also beset with limitations.

During 1871 the Home Rule movement continued to spread in Ireland and Britain. By the close of the year most large English towns with considerable Irish populations had hosted at least one Home Rule meeting. Heinrick took an active role in Home Rule organization. On 30 January he made an exhaustive speech at a banquet for A.M. Sullivan held in Liverpool.[25] He attended the St. Patrick's Day festivities in Birmingham where he spoke on the home rule theme.[26] Stirrings were evident elsewhere. At the St. Patrick's Day celebrations John Ferguson pointed out that the Irish had no influence in Glasgow but were on the verge of being organized.[27] At the end of May he announced:

> it is proposed to organise the Glasgow Irish so that their influence may be felt all over the world and in local matters which concern themselves alone. There is an Irish population here numbering probably 150,000. Some think that very little effort would give them half a dozen seats in the Town Council.[28]

Ferguson suggested that the Irish were capable of electing their own MP as well, but, "whether these calculations are Utopian or correct, organisation is an end as well as a means. It is educational and improving, and it indicates life". In October at a Home Rule meeting in Hackney a key speaker observed that the "great object of the London and the other branch associations would be to organise the Irish vote so as to use it in turning contested elections, and thus endeavour to tempt one or more of the candidates to support Home Rule principles".[29] In November Butt attended a demonstration in Glasgow for the purpose of establishing a branch of the Home Government Association. In his speech Butt emphasized the electoral function of the immigrants:

> I think the Irish people in places like Glasgow could give us a little help in bringing the influence of their votes to bear upon the Scotch

> members, and there ought to be, wherever there are Irish people, associations formed for the express purpose of obtaining justice for Ireland, and associating the Irish people in the different localities.[30]

As the year concluded *The Nation* commented favourably on the growth of Home Rule patriotism in England.[31]

Between January and July 1872 Home Rule branches in Britain mushroomed. At the opening of the year the first meeting of branches was held in Liverpool with a reported 2,500 in attendance at the public session.[32] The Rev. J.A. Galbraith and A.M. Sullivan from the Home Government Association in Dublin were present along with Heinrick and Denvir. In the following month it was asserted that the establishment of a Home Rule branch "had given to the Irishmen of Bradford for the first time a true and real centre of union and cohesion".[33] In May the chairman of a meeting in London stressed the critical work ahead particularly that of organizing the community.[34] He projected a future where the Irish in the metropolis would wield as much power as they did in New York. Shortly afterwards at an Irish meeting in London, Butt urged his listeners to vote only for Home Rulers at the next election.[35] Even as the series of articles was being published, there were numerous reports of Irish activism throughout England. One from Islington noted that:

> the Brothers of St. Vincent de Paul [were] to aid them in obtaining copies of voters' register, and supplying the association with the names of all the Catholic voters upon it so that the committee could call upon them. By these means they were not only rapidly extending their organisation throughout England, but by the aid of the fathers they were getting to know and keep an account of every man's views on the subject.[36]

Mid 1872, thus, was a moment of rising Home Rule activity in Britain when the potential of the community was gaining wide recognition. Heinrick was an obvious and appropriate choice to write the series and *The Nation*, under A.M. Sullivan, a periodical which had an interest in the immigrants. Yet a series of such length remains something of a puzzle. It appears to be the longest sustained piece of the type published in *The Nation* between 1867 and 1891, perhaps the only one so extensive ever to appear in the journal. Furthermore, the newspaper never commissioned a subsequent investigation of the Irish community. There must be a suspicion that Sullivan engaged Heinrick, in part at least, as a means of providing a modest income in the wake of the failure of the *Irish Vindicator* and to assist his work of rousing Home Rule enthusiasm in England.

As a social investigator, Heinrick had virtues and defects. He was, of course, a partisan of the home rule movement and not a detached observer. Yet he was also a generally honest surveyor who did not ignore or deflate the weaknesses of the Irish community. His series belongs to the "tour" genre but Heinrick was certainly not a Young, Defoe, de Tocqueville or Cobbett nor were his skills of social analysis comparable to those of Mayhew, Booth or Roundtree. Heinrick was a modestly talented journalist who conceived and prepared the articles quickly to a narrow remit. He was not systematic, his sources of information far from exhaustive and methodology unimpressive. Heinrick's survey cannot be passed off as a near classic study which has been lost. Its importance is two-fold – as an investigation of a group which has been neglected, and, because the survey falls into a vital time gap between the flood of Famine era refugees and the second wave of Irish emigration consequent on the agrarian depression of the later Victorian age.

Heinrick's survey was limited to England. He did not extend coverage to to Wales nor Scotland, where the proportion of Irish was actually greater than in England. *The Nation* never commissioned a subsequent series on the northern kingdom. Heinrick's study was the product of his own observations, discussions with leading figures in the immigrant community, notably priests and home rule supporters, and assorted second-hand accounts. He visited many, though not all, of the places described. The most valuable sections of his topographical survey were those on the midlands and north where his investigation was largely a first-hand account. His comments on Leicester, Birmingham, the Black Country, Lancashire, Yorkshire and the north east are superior to other sections. He did not personally travel through the south, outside London, or south west nor, as he made clear, did he visit the Potteries. Thus, the series is uneven in detail and insight. The patchy character pertains to typology as well. Heinrick's essential concern was the political organization or its potential strength and the religious health of the immigrants. In order to assess his particular interest he was obliged to treat the economic, social and moral condition of the people, for which he provided valuable evidence, but they were not usually his prime concern. Heinrick's comparisons between the various towns surveyed were often illuminating; fortunately he was not a very acute commentator on distinctions within the same place or of graduations in a single enclave. While his study adds texture to an appreciation of the Irish experience, it lacks sophistication. Heinrick never succeeded in lifting more than a corner of the veil which shrouded, and has continued to shroud the Irish in Britain.

No part of the survey illustrates the limitations or completely disappoints expectations than that on London. Heinrick had after all resided in the metropolis and had good reason to give London appropriate attention. He expended considerable printers' ink on the capital. He devoted three articles which had to be split over four issues to an analysis of the Irish there. It was the most extended part of the whole enterprise. Heinrick had almost nothing fresh or of insight to write about the metropolis. He depended heavily on an old article by Father Todd and his own accretions were essentially impressionistic.[37] Though he attempted to give due weight to every aspect of Irish life in London the commentary lacks precision. He noted, for example:

> there are probably, a quarter of a million of people resident in London of Irish birth and parentage, and these more nearly represent the nation at home than do the Irish residents of any other town or city on earth. Here we have the very extremes of Irish society mixing and commingling in the rush and roar of life that rolls for ever in the haunts of fashion, the busy marts, and the crowded thoroughfares of this all absorbing centre of life.[38]

He emphasized that there was a substantial middle and artisan class capable of setting an example and providing leadership for the masses of Irish. "These classes combined," he wrote, "constitute an Irish power in London which in point of intellect, patriotic earnestness, energetic manhood, and fidelity to faith and fatherland, are not excelled by any section of the Irish people on earth".[39] Irish intellect, he proclaimed, "dominates in the studios, shines in the closet, and educates and rules in the press".[40] He then catalogued a list of eminent Irishmen and their achievements. In the press world especially Irish figures were prominent for

> there is not a newspaper in London without its one, two, three and four Irish writers and Irish reporters on its staff – indeed, Irish reporters are not alone numerous, but are the best and the ablest who supply the daily papers with the Court and Parliamentary records of the day.[41]

Yet, he decried, "in too many instances, as the mere mercenaries of the English interest – they were prepared to turn, metaphorically, on the spit their own kith and kin, at an hour's notice, at the usual stipulated price of two or three guineas an article".[42] His theme that the capital was a Mecca for the ambitious not just of the poor and that the immigrants there had the makings of a complete class structure commands confidence, though is scarcely an unusual analysis. Regrettably, Heinrick's discussion does not advance beyond hyperbole.

Although the survey was conducted topographically, and has as noted, particular utility for certain places, its chief interest for many people is Heinrick's analysis of immigrant demography, social characteristics, occupational patterns, religious participation, political potential and similar issues. While his observations often fail to convince, they nevertheless merit attention. Heinrick's attempt, for instance, to define the Irish community raises a fundamental difficulty. Who were the Irish? An examination of the survey must suggest that Heinrick was unsure or at least inconsistent in his answer. He was at some pains to argue that the investigation transcended his own confessional community though in practice he treated Irish and Catholic as virtually synonymous. He was also determined to assess the community in its full sense including the descendants of the Irish-born as well as the immigrants. As is well-known, the British census which recorded only place of birth, necessarily under-estimated Irish numbers. Heinrick, like other Irish observers, sought to identify the ethnic groups as a whole, and not just those born on the opposite shore of St. George's Channel. On the basis of an aggregation of Irish numbers in each district, he concluded that the ethnic community totalled approximately 2,500,000. Heinrick's reckoning was a gross exaggeration. Nationalists' regularly asserted that the number was about 2,000,000, also a very considerable inflation. Any attempted calculation must be inexact, though the number surely was no greater than 1,000,000 or at the extreme 1,250,000, that is, less than half of Heinrick's estimate.

Heinrick's figure is a vivid reminder that no readily accurate count of the Irish existed in the nineteenth century and none is available even now. Before dismissing his estimate out of hand, it is worthwhile inquiring what he meant by Irish. Clearly Heinrick included everyone of Irish origin, Protestants as well as Catholics, children, grand children, and the scion of mixed ancestry. He counted, then, everyone possible whether they wished inclusion in the Irish comunity or felt an identity with it. On that basis, his arithmetic is less absurd though it also is wholly spurious in defining effective Irish identity. Heinrick's survey, shows the difficulty of ascertaining who the Irish were.

His calculation of community size revealed the degree to which the Irish had been integrated and assimilated. He noted that approximately one-eighth were lost to faith and fatherland on or shortly after arrival in their adopted land. Heinrick, in fact, emphasized the impact of intermarriage and upward mobility. Of the first, he complained:

> their defection is greatly facilitated by intermarriage with English families, and the consequent conformity which follows. The loss,

> numerically, could be borne; but the misfortune is, that the class which feeds this defection is the class whose means would enable them to be of the greatest benefit to their country and their kindred did they not thus fall away from the standard of patriotic duty.[43]

Heinrick identified "three causes at work which are gradually sapping the strength of Irish communities".[44] Those were emigration overseas, particularly to America, people "who, having attained to comparative prosperity, wish to forget their nativity, and in all things conform to English thought and English habit"; and the dissolute. "There is", he suggested darkly;

> a constant decrease of an eighth of the Irish population in England from all those causes; and hence it is contended that as this propoprtion is nearly equal to the natural increase of the people, it is only a question of time till the entire Irish element is drawn into the life of the English people.[45]

Heinrick believed that the only salvation of the Irish as a distinct people was "isolation" and a function of nationalist politics was to separate them from the influences of the host. In the short-term Heinrick's prophesy was betrayed by the further waves of immigrants; in the longer run his gloomy prediction proved right: the Irish neither wished nor were able to hold themselves aloof from their new land. If Heinrick's statistics are dubious, his attempt to come to grips with the perimeters of Irishness has lasting value.

A focus of the survey was the religion, morals and education of the community. If his conclusions lack novelty for what has become probably the most fully researched side of Irish life, he succeeded in contributing a dimension to the discussion, notably the differentiation between various places. Heinrick paid tribute to the moral fibre of the vast majority who resisted the temptations around them. But the battle against satanic forces was prodigious. As he pointed out, "there is a perpetual epidemic of vice in London. Irish virtue is the only prophylatic which resists it".[46] Yet Heinrick lamented that some succumbed with a consequence that:

> there are thousands – tens of thousands of the Irish people in London alone who are lost – lost irretrievably. There is no gainsaying it, and to shut one's eyes to it and see only the good, without estimating the evil and the loss, would be the merest criminal folly. Our people are crushed, physically debased, and morally ruined by the dreaded circumstances almost inseparable from their lot. The poverty which drove them from home is their evil genius abroad. There own improvidence – it is only fair to add – in some instances lead to their degradation and destruction. The drink demon is the fatal phantom that lures thousands to their doom. Drink – drink is the crime and the curse of Irishmen in this country. It is the stigma which of all others is the most fatal to their character, the cloud that hides the brilliant lustre of their many virtues.

His own views on the drink question are unknown but stress upon the problems inflicted by alcohol chimed with the outlook of A.M. Sullivan, a fervent temperance advocate. Heinrick was incensed about the unsavoury impact of an alien environment on the young, notably girls, for as he averred:

> the associations, particularly for the young, are most pernicious. The children grow up breathing an atmosphere of impurity from the first, by which their whole moral nature is vitiated. The young girl fresh from Ireland is forced, from her poverty, on arrival into positions most detrimental to her safety. The lower middle-class, the small shopkeepers – often devoid of religion and morals – or the still lower and more demoralised Jews of Spitalfields and Whitechapel, are the chief employers of the unsophsticated Irish girl when she first arrives in London.[47]

"Notwithstanding the superior spiritual gifts and virtue of our race", he concluded, "the percentage of the fallen is fearful."[48]

There were some exceptional black-spots on the moral landscape. In the Black Country, despite generally good wage rates, money was too often "squandered in the most prodigal folly".[49] Despite the deplorable state of the Irish in much of the region, around Bilston, Oldbury and Willenhall, he found the moral condition more satisfactory. Elsewhere the pattern was varied. In Burton the situation was even more squalid. Though matters were better in Nottingham, "the stamp of vice is too plainly on the community'.[50] Of Hull, Heinrick winced, "the general moral state of the town is low, and the condition of the Irish population corresponds with its surroundings".[51] In Bradford and Halifax "though there is much to be seen only to be deplored – the state of the Irish population is satisfactory".[52] But in the north east, he pointed out, the problem was less severe. In Newcastle upon Tyne "the moral condition of the Irish people stands high when contrasted to other towns".[53] In the communities stretching along the Tyne moral life approximated to that of Newcastle. Heinrick had a three-fold explanation for the discrepancies he catalogued: the Irish followed local *mores*, particularly where they were subjected to intregrationist pressure; the provision and effectiveness of the Catholic Church in various places; and the degree of ethnic unity and cohesion maintained. "Isolation", he contended, "so far as possible, is the safety and salvation of the Irish people . . ."[54] In contrast, "social intercourse . . . is a curse rather than a blessing to the Irish people".[55]

If Heinrick's treatment of the moral state of the Irish contains an implicit criticism of the Church, his direct discussion of religious provision was deferential. As could be expected from a series published in *The Nation*, the Church received generous coverage. In certain places the number of churches were enumerated, even listing their names, while for others only a general comment on the state – almost always favourable – of religious life was the extent of Heinrick's assessment. Unfortunately, he did not probe the question of why the Church was more successful in some instances than others in halting moral backsliding. He did confirm the remarkable progress of the Church in erecting suitable and extensive buildings financed mainly from parishoners subscriptions only a little more than twenty years after the Famine. However, Heinrick's pietistic attitude and suspension of critical faculties gives the description of religion a wearisome character.

The survey examined the provision of education from two perspectives: as an avenue for the next generation's upward mobility; and, a device for solidifying the Irish community, protecting its morals and insuring cohesion. Heinrick was more effective in detailing the quantity than the quality of education provision. In most towns he found the numbers of Catholic schools and teachers adequate. In London, however, he noted a short-fall of 5,000 school places.[56] Heinrick's obsequious attitude to religious authority was an inhibition to a thorough critical investigation, a failure that must be counted as a disappointment in view of the author's own background in Catholic schools.

Related to the general condition of the community is the issue of Irish criminality. Contemporary British comment dwelled on the apparent high rate of crime perpetuated by the Irish. Recent research has confirmed the impression that they were responsible for crime at rates disproportionate to their numbers.[57] The survey of 1872 did not tackle the issue in depth. Heinrick on occasion noted where the Irish were drawn into, or relatively free of, criminality. Of Leicester, for instance, he observed that:

> they are eminently free from the taint of ordinary crime is attested by the fact . . . that on the criminal calandar for the whole of Leicestershire there is not a single Irish name, and within the borough jurisdiction but three or four, for offences which are the merest trifles – cases of petty larceny or offences arising out of drunken brawls.[58]

But, similar remarks were often too infrequent to afford more than a promising line of inquiry.

Possibly the most valuable parts deal with an occupational profile of the Irish. There has been little attempt at systematic analysis of how the exiles fared in the employment market, whether their progeny achieved upward mobility and at what rate embourgeoisiement took place. Heinrick's interest in Irish employment prospects arose in part from a realization that "the political power of a people is, in a great measure, dependent on their social condition".[59] Also, because regularity of wages and stability of residence were crucial in qualification for the ballot under the Reform Act of 1867. Society's residuum remained disfranchised. Irish participation in politics was therefore linked to their place in the occupational structure.

At all points in the years between 1845 and 1922 the Irish were located disproportionately among the labouring poor. Frederich Engels in the 1840s observed that in occupations which required strength rather than skill were "especially overcrowded with Irishmen; hand weavers, bricklayers, porters, jobbers and such workers count hordes of Irishmen among their number, and the pressure of this race has done much to depress wages and lower the working class"[60] In 1881 it was claimed that 82 per cent of the Irish-born were day labourers while the census report for 1891 analyzed a sample of Liverpool employments and emphasized that they were "engaged in the rougher kinds of unskilled labour, the proportions of artisans and of dealers of all kinds and grades being very small".[61] Denvir made an effort to counter that typical portrait when he pointed to the substantial upward mobility of his compatriots.[62] Modern writers, while recognizing Denvir's point, have confirmed that Irish advancement was painfully slow.[63] Moreover, it has been asserted that upward mobility was limited particularly in the decades after 1850, only gaining momentum towards the end of the century. In Liverpool, for instance, the Irish encountered exceptional difficulty in moving into skilled jobs. Heinrick's investigation was revealing in two respects: he demonstrated differences over space and generations, and, he attempted for certain places to place Irish wage levels in a local context.

As might be anticipated, his evidence is most precise for the midlands and the north. In his discussion of Leicester he noted, "with few exceptions they are literally the hewers of wood and drawers of water".[64] He attributed their lowly position to the fact that "the Irishman comes unskilled to England, and hence his destiny has doomed him to the most dreary drudgery".[65] Yet he pointed out, "the wage-rate is good, and but for the one vice of drunkenness – almost the only vice which degrades and disgraces our people all through England – the social condition of the Irish in Leicester would rapidly improve". In his assessment of the city he knew best, Birmingham, Heinrick alleged:

> there is to be found a larger percentage of the Irish people who are trained to skilled and artistic workmanship than in most of the other English towns; and here, as in all other cases where Irish taste and genius are cultivated, their peculiar adaptability for the higher kinds of manual art is evident.[66]

Still, he conceded, "the great body of the people earn their bread by the severest toil". Very significantly, though, he observed that "chiefly the young have been trained to skilled labour . . ." He contrasts Birmingham with the Black Country where in the former:

> there are various trades and callings in which the Irish people – and particularly the young – are trained to skilled and artistic labour. In the latter, the coal pit, the iron mine, the pit-head labour, and the furnace, furnish the chief sources of employ for the people, both English and Irish. The Irish people, in proportion to their numbers, supply a fair quota to the ranks of the more skilled employees in the manufactures; but the great bulk of Irish labour is either confined to the occupations mentioned or employed by railway companies, builders, etc., in the lowest and most laborious positions, and at a wage rate considerably below what can be obtained by those employed at the mines or in the works connected with the iron-manufactures.[67]

Within the region marked differences were apparent. At Wednesbury which had a substantial Irish concentration they "earn very high wages (indeed, the highest in the whole district) . . ."[68] Also, he noted the shifting pattern of employment. In Black Country mining, though given the rougher kinds of work, they were no longer barred from employment as in the recent past. In Dudley the Irish received "good wages, and, in proportion to their numbers, there are more skilled artisans in this than in the other towns of the district".[69] Heinrick insisted, "there is also a fair number of men who have raised themselves out of the ranks of labour, and are pushing onwards to comfort and competence".

His differential analysis was confirmed in other districts. At

Walsall and Wolverhampton the Irish were "chiefly of the labouring class, but all earning good wages and were comparatively well-to-do".[70] At Burton, in contrast, their remuneration was low and condition very degraded. In Chesterfield the average Irish earnings were reported to be 24s a week.[71] In Yorkshire, though, few Irish were found outside the ranks of the unskilled but in most places they received adequate wages. For Lancashire the picture remained broadly consistent to that of its eastern neighbour. Yet within Lancashire distinctions between towns were important. Heinrick's comparison of St. Helen's, Widnes and Wigan made his case. In the first, he calculated that nearly a third of the population was Irish and:

> they are for the most part unskilled labourers employed in the chemical and glass work for which the town is noted. It will be easily understood that the Irish in coming here have had to commence in the lowest and most laborious places, and if they rise at all must do so in virtue of their superior power of physical endurance and high mental and moral energy. Without these qualities they could not have risen. That they possessed them is proven by the fact that many have risen to the position of foremen, some to the post of managers, and a few have become manufacturers.[72]

At Widnes "the occupation of the people . . . is nearly the same as in St Helen's with the exception of the glass works. Here the occupation is chiefly confined to chemical or 'alkali' works. There is a larger proportion of the Irish people here confined to labour . . ."[73] In Wigan, which had the highest proportion of Irish of any English town:

> nearly all are labourers or factory hands. A few have worked their way into the ranks of the lower middle class, and a still larger number are small traders and skilled artisans. In the surrounding district many are employed in the pits and iron works, usually in positions where labour is hardest and wages least. Nearly half the pit-men in the neighbouring coal and iron works are now Irish, though till recently, the English miner refused to work beside the Irishman, and hatred and hostility marked nearly every relation of the men of the one nationaliy to those of the other.[74]

For Liverpool Heinrick attempted to enumerate the Irish in various occupations. Outside London, Liverpool had the widest diversity and probably the largest middle-class. Heinrick believed that "from one-fifth to one-sixth of the Irish population . . . are above the ranks of ordinary toil . . ."[75] In his investigation of Newcastle upon Tyne, he attempted a similar exercise. He estimated:

> there are among them 400 business men of various grades and conditions, and over 4,000 skilled artisans, that is about 5,000 – or nearly one in six – who have worked upwards from the severest drudgery to a condition of comparative prosperity.[76]

Near Newcastle, in places such as North and South Shields, the Irish fared much as they did in the region's chief entrepôt.

Several conclusions about occupation patterns are evident in the survey. Obviously, most Irish remained anchored in base work but wages rates differed by town and industry. Upward mobility, especially for the second generation, was observable but tied to local circumstances. Where more skilled work was available, the Irish found fewer barriers to progress. Irish employment appears to have been determined less by their absolute or proportionate numbers in a district, than by the character of the place where they settled. Unfortunately Heinrick did not explore the question of why individual Irish selected particular destinations for settlement in Britain, or the extent of internal migration after arrival or over subsequent generations. Nevertheless, the survey documented the degree of stability which the Famine era migrants had achieved within a little more than two decades, the extent of adaption and their shifting position within the employment market.

The *raison d'être* for the articles was an analysis of the present and future impact of the Irish on the outcome of elections. He painted a glowing prospect but acknowledged that almost everywhere that power was unrealized. By and large, he did not attribute the current state of affairs to institutional or social barriers in the host community. If the Irish suffered unduly, as they did at Wigan, from a bias in the franchise and registration regulations, Heinrick thought that in most towns their entitlement to the ballot did not differ markedly from the English. He believed that one in seven of the whole Irish number was qualified for the franchise. Irish weakness, Heinrick, suggested arose from an absence of organization. He saw the remedy in "unity, organization, and action".[77] Endemic poor organization had to be overcome. In certain places, Heinrick insisted, the root of the difficulty lay in an insufficient Irish middle-class to provide essential leadership, though, as he noted, its existence in London did not produce cohesive organization. He asserted that where a middle-class capable of giving local leadership was deficient, the void must be filled by regular visits from prominent men in the national movement. "In many places in England some such course is necessary if all the constituents of our power are to be combined and made effective", he pleaded.[78] Politics, Heinrick asserted, had a key purpose of binding the Irish together, giving them power, respect, self-confidence, and a prophylactic to resist the insidious effects of English culture. In Manchester, he noted:

> the want of Irish representation in local affairs is due, in fact, to the absence of Irish organisation – the want of an *Irish Party* in the town, which could command respect for the Irish people as a body, and be ready on every occasion to champion their cause and advance their interests. The Irish people in any town in England, while divided into sections, and attached to English parties, are practically powerless. It is only when united, and acting as a body, that they secure influence and respect. In Manchester the organisation essential to political success would also promote local influence and social respect.[79]

Political action for Heinrick had a multi-functional purpose. He saw in it the device for unifying an ethnic community which, even in 1872, was on the verge of disintegration.

If the survey contains comparatively few surprises for a present-day audience, it nonetheless provides useful background to a neglected era of the exiles' experience. Heinrick, above all, showed that easy generalizations should be eschewed for what characterized the Irish most was differences over time and space.

Some, though certainly not all, were an isolated group on the fringe of English society; more were well along the path towards integration and assimilation. The survey reveals the Irish as lacking key requisites for behaving as an effective ethnic bloc.

Curiously the articles evoked only modest contemporary response. Publication of the series did however contribute towards elevating Heinrick's reputation in the years after 1872. He soon became a frequent and popular speaker at Irish demonstrations in England. With the founding of the Home Rule League in November 1873, Heinrick was appointed as one of the paid officials, working in both Ireland and also at Westminster until his discharge became necessary due to an absence of funds. While employed by the League, he wrote a pamphlet titled, "What is Home Rule?" which was published in Denvir's Penny Illustrated Library in March 1874. *The Nation* welcomed its appearance with the limp commendation, "while we should wish him to be a little less oratorical, and more explanatory in these pages, we are sure that there is no friend of the Home Rule cause who peruses his essay but will deem it a serviceable publication".[80] "The Irish in England" was also reissued as a pamphlet in August 1874 in Denvir's series.[81] No copy of either pamphlet appears to have survived. When the Home Rule Confederation of Great Britain began publication of its own weekly newspaper, *The United Irishmen*, in June 1875, Heinrick and Denvir were the editors. This journal, too, collapsed in February 1877 after continuous bouts of fiscal difficulty.[82] Heinrick then dropped from sight, dying in early October 1877 of a lingering illness. He was in his forty-seventh year and had returned to school teaching in Birmingham. His death was marked only by a brief obituary in the nationalist press. Though he left a widow and children and was reported to be poor, there was no public subscription for them as frequently happened on the death of a nationalist stalwart. Both Heinrick and the survey quickly passed into obscurity. A.M. Sullivan made no mention of either in his successful, *New Ireland*,[83] which chronicled the rise of the Home Rule movement. Denvir also ignored the series and made no reference to Heinrick, though the two men had been close associates in the 1870s. Hugh Heinrick's moment as an Irish celebrity was brief and uncommemorated.

Only Denvir's *The Irish in Britain*, first published exactly two decades later, was comparable. Neither the articles by W.G. Todd in the *Dublin Review* or the four articles in *The Nation*, both published in 1856, were extensive.[84] The latter had in fact been inspired by the visit of the Rev. George Montgomery of Wednesbury to Dublin, and was restricted to the West Midlands. Heinrick's survey was both the most extensive and intensive investigation of the Irish community prior to publication of Denvir's volume. Even that, though in total of far greater length than Heinrick's articles, only devoted the final eighty-three pages specifically to the Irish in Britain. Despite the title, most of the volume was a chronology of the national struggle in Ireland. Denvir's book, unlike Heinrick's survey, extended to Wales and Scotland. It depended heavily on official, mainly census, information. The two studies should be seen as complementary. Both Heinrick and Denvir raised queries about the nature of Irish life which, even now, await answers. Publication of the survey of 1872 may extend appreciation of the Irish experience and stimulate further research in a field that has only begun to attract interest.

[1] J.E. Handley, *The Irish in Scotland, 1798-1845* (Cork 1943); *The Irish in Modern Scotland* (Cork 1947).

[2] E.P.M. Wollaston, "The Irish Nationalist Movement in Great Britain, 1886-1908", University of London, M.A. (1958); H.W. Benjamin, "The London Irish: A Study in Political Activism, 1870-1910", Princeton University Ph.D. (1976); R.J. Cooter, "The Irish in County Durham and Newcastle, *c.* 1840-1880", University of Durham M.A. thesis (1972). See also, Roger Swift, "The Outcast Irish in the British Victorian City: Problems and Perspectives", *Irish Historical Studies*, xxv (May 1987), pp.264-76.

[3] *The Nation*, 13 October 1877; *Freeman's Journal*, 10 October 1877; *Ulster Examiner*, 11 October 1877.

[4] *Irish Vindicator*, 30 September 1871.

[5] Maureen Hartigan, Alan O'Day and Roland Quinault, "Irish Terrorism in Britain: A Comparison Between the Activities of the Fenians in the 1860s and those of Republican Groups since 1972" in Yonah Alexander and Alan O'Day (eds.), *Ireland's Terrorist Dilemma* (Dordrecht 1986), p.50.

[6] *The Nation*, 22 June 1867.
[7] *Ibid.*, 12 October 1867.
[8] *Ibid.*, 6 June 1868.
[9] *Ibid.*, 18 May 1867.
[10] *Ibid.*, 26 June 1869.
[11] *Ibid.*, 11 June 1870.
[12] *Ibid.*, 28 May 1870.
[13] *Ibid.*, 18 June 1870.
[14] *Ibid.*, 16 July 1870.
[15] *Ibid.*, 1 October 1870; see also, 24 September.
[16] *Ibid.*, 15 October 1870.
[17] *Ibid.*, 1 October 1870.
[18] *Ibid.*, 17 December 1870.
[19] Based on David Fitzpatrick's chapters in the forthcoming *New History of Ireland.*
[20] Lynn Hollen Lees, *Exiles of Erin* (Manchester 1979), p.58.
[21] David Large, "The Irish in Bristol in 1851: A Census Enumeration", in Roger Swift and Sheridan Gilley (eds.), *The Irish in the Victorian City* (London 1985), p.38.
[22] Colin G. Pooley, "The Residential Segregation of Migrant Communities in mid-Victorian Liverpool", *Transaction of the Institute of British Geographers*, New Series, ii (2, 1977), pp.364-82; Richard Lawton, "Irish Migration to England and Wales in the Mid-Nineteenth Century", *Irish Geography*, iv (1959), pp.35-56; J. Papworth, "The Irish in Liverpool 1835-72", University of Liverpool Ph.D. (1981); Paul Laxton, "Neighbourhoods or Ghettos? Some Considerations of the Irish Districts of English Cities in the Nineteenth Century", unpublished paper delivered to a joint meeting of the British Academy and the Royal Irish Academy in London on 30 September 1986.
[23] Large, *op.cit.*, p.41.
[24] *Ibid*, p.51.
[25] *The Nation*, 11 February 1871.
[26] *Ibid.*, 18 March 1871.
[27] *Ibid.*
[28] *Ibid.*, 3 June 1871.
[29] *Ibid.*, 28 October 1871.
[30] *Ibid.*, 18 November 1871.
[31] *Ibid.*, 23 December 1871.
[32] *Ibid.*, 6 January 1872.
[33] *Ibid.*, 17 February 1872.
[34] *Ibid.*, 25 May 1872.
[35] *Ibid.*, 15 June 1872.
[36] *Ibid.*, 24 August 1872.
[37] W.G. Todd, "The Irish in England", *Dublin Review*, lxxxii (December

1856), pp.470-521; reprinted with additions, *The Irish in England* (London, 1857).

[38] p.2.

[39] p.8.

[40] p.10.

[41] p.11.

[42] *Ibid.*

[43] p.127.

[44] *Ibid.*

[45] p.128.

[46] p.27.

[47] pp.28-29.

[48] p.31.

[49] p.49.

[50] p.64.

[51] p.66.

[52] p.74.

[53] p.120.

[54] p.53.

[55] p.51.

[56] p.32.

[57] David Fitzpatrick's chapters in the forthcoming *New History of Ireland.*

[58] p.40.

[59] p.90.

[60] Friedrich Engels, *The Condition of the Working-Class in England* (Reprint, London 1969), p.125.

[61] p.192; K.S. Inglis, *Churches and the Working Classes in Victorian England* (London 1963), p.193; *Census Report, 1891,* pp.62-63.

[62] John Denvir, *The Irish in Britian* (2nd ed., London 1894), pp.389-462.

[63] Lees, *Exiles of Erin*, p.242; P.J. Waller, *Democracy & Sectarianism* (Liverpool 1981), pp.1-206.

[64] p.39.

[65] *Ibid.*

[66] p.42.

[67] p.46.

[68] p.49.

[69] p.53.

[70] pp.53-54.

[71] p.57.

[72] p.65.

[73] p.113.

[74] p.99.

[75] p.91.

[76] p.119.

[77] p.95.
[78] p.77.
[79] p.84.
[80] *The Nation*, 21 March 1874.
[81] *Ibid.*, 8 August 1874.
[82] *United Irishman*, 18 November 1876; John Denvir to Isaac Butt, 24 and 27 August 1876, I. Butt Papers, National Library of Ireland, Ms 8698 (36).
[83] *The Nation*, 13 October 1877; *Freeman's Journal*, 10 October 1877; *Ulster Examiner*, 11 October 1877.
[84] A.M. Sullivan, *New Ireland* (London 1877); *The Nation*, 17 May, 7 June, 14 June, 28 June 1856; Todd, *op.cit.*

Letter I

London, 3rd July, 1872

To follow in the footsteps of our race and kindred, whom the evil effects of an alien rule at home have made wanderers and sojourners in the land of the oppressor; to point out their fate, fortunes, and destiny in the home of their adoption; to trace the influence they exercise on the religious, the moral, the social, and political state of the people among whom they reside; to indicate the force of the new life they have introduced into England, and the broad political revival to which the closer intercourse of Englishmen and Irishmen has given rise, with the political consequences likely to rise therefrom – in fact, to gather facts and materials to show as nearly as may be the actual strength and condition of the Irish in England, the force they can exercise in aid of the national cause at home, and their general influence on imperial politics and imperial destiny – this is the task which the commission with which I am charged imposes on me, and to this I propose to devote myself with whatever ability I can command, and with all the affectionate zeal of one whom the call of duty summons to a labour of love. It is the first time that such a task has been undertaken – the first time that the motherland, solicitous for the weal of all her offspring, has sent into England to inquire after the fate of the scattered ones of the household. In the United States of America we have an Irish nation more powerful than that which exists in the cradle of our race. In Canada, in Australia, in New Zealand, and at the Cape, are large and prosperous Irish communities rapidly assuming the leading position in the gradual development of those colonies into independent nations. In England the position of our people is more circumscribed, and their apparent destiny different. What that position really is – how it operates in and influences society – and the duty and destiny of our brethren in England in relation to the great national struggle now in progress at home – are points that shall claim special attention in the progress of the commission which has been entrusted to me.

I deemed it most fitting that a mission to the Irish in England should begin in London, and hence from this point I transmit the result of my first observations. Here, in this great fevered, restless, heartless community, are congregated together possibly the largest number of our people to be found in any one spot on earth out of their own land. There are, probably, a quarter of a million people resident in London of Irish birth and parentage, and these more nearly represent the nation at home than do the Irish residents of any other town or city on earth. Here we have the very extremes of Irish society mixing and commingling in the rush and roar of life that rolls for ever in the haunts of fashion, the busy marts, and the crowded thoroughfares of this all-absorbing centre of life. Here are to be met the tyrant and the victim – the oppressor and the oppressed. Here the fruits of the hard and bitter toil of the Irish peasant are daily and nightly squandered in the haunts of fashion and of vice – while the wretched victims of the system which makes London the sweating-house of Irish wealth exists in squalid misery in some obscure and unhealthy East-end court, pining for the soft sunlight and health-giving breezes of his native hillside. In the precincts of Mayfair and the Parks by day – in the still more questionable associations of the Haymarket at night – the pink of fashion – the proudest among the proud – are to be seen the Irish aristocracy in their gay and splendid equipages, or their juniors among the dashing and fashionable *roues* who make the night hideous with their orgies. In the neighbourhood of Whitechapel or Bethnal Green is congregated the vast army of Irish toil or Irish misery whom the accursed Land system rooted out of their happy homesteads by the Barrow or the Blackwater, the Foyle or the Shannon, the Liffey or the Slaney – some of them struggling manfully and hopefully against the bitter decrees of destiny – others sinking broken-hearted in the strife – withering like plants of another clime – fading beneath the inclemency of strange skies; and, worse than this, others sinking lower still into that worst and lowest state of all – that lowest deep beneath which even imagination cannot conceive a lower – that sink of moral pollution in which wallow the lowest dregs of English society. Into this vortex of vice hundreds are drawn who sink to rise no more. Had we statistics of the destruction of Irish life and the wreck of Irish morals consequent in the migration of the people to England, the record would be something fearful to contemplate. And yet our people are in every moral attribute infinitely superior to the race among whom their lot is cast. I shall have more to add in a future paper on this head, and wish for the present to confine myself to a contrast of the phases of Irish life to be found in London and a reference to the Irish influences which aid the Imperial system in accomplishing results alike destructive of prosperity at home and of the lives and morals of the expatriated people. I will merely say, then, that poverty more than any other social cause tends to the moral degradation of the Irish people in the English towns, and particularly in London. Poverty, the curse from which the Irishman fled at home, too often sits with him as an evil destiny abroad. He comes poor, he has to settle amongst the poor of the English towns – that is, amongst the most vicious of the worst classes in English society – where his generous and impressionable nature too readily assumes the mask and manner of his surroundings, till the vice which he abhorred previously becomes by degrees less hideous and repellant, and custom blunts the finer feelings and higher spiritual and moral attainments of his nature. Indeed, considering the associations which surround the Irish people on their arrival in England, the marvel is that so few should sink in passing through the fiery furnace of iniquity into which their poverty flings them. The people of Ireland can form but a very inadequate notion of the demoralising influences against which their brethren in England have to struggle. In England it is terribly manifest, and the dread loss too palpable to be ignored. And yet there are today over two millions of the Irish people resident in Great Britain – in mental and physical qualities the equals of any – in morality and religion incomparably superior to the people among whom they live – constituting an Irish nation distinct and peculiar, amid all the evil influences of English social life.

I point to the extremes of Irish social life in London not without a purpose. The prodigality of the landlord class and the poverty of the poor East-end outcasts are but evidences of cause and effect – the one of which must be arrested before the other can be checked. Till an Irish Parliament either holds out sufficient inducements to the Irish landlords to reside at home, or imposes a penalty on absenteeism, Irish wealth will be squandered in England. Till the same influence develops the resources and promotes the manufacturing industry of Ireland, the poverty-stricken will fly the land. The poorer and weaker of these as a rule find their way into England to become "hewers of wood and drawers of water", and to add to the moral loss I have pointed out and which all must deplore. This is not less a question for the consideration of the divine and the moralist than for the politician and the nationalist. It is as much a question of faith and morals as of nationality. The system that not alone destroys the spirit and resources of a nation, but that in its consequences degrades and demoralises its victims, deserves the unqualified condemnation of all good men. That the system of English rule in Ireland has done, and continues to do this, no one can deny. To see and understand this in its worst aspect one must see and understand the terrible wreck wrought among the Irish in England by the evil associations almost inseparable from their lot; and seeing and understanding this, it is difficult to conceive how any sentiment, save that of the most unqualified condemnation, can be entertained in reference to a rule which after seven centuries of bloody and brutal oppression, while professing to have changed its spirit and appliances culminates, in such disastrous social and moral results as these.

Between the sybarites of society who squander Irish wealth in the English metropolis, and the poor crushed and heartbroken victims who perish unnoticed by the wayside of life, there is in London, as in nearly all the large towns in England, an immense force of Irish life, energy, and intelligence, which, if organised and united, would constitute a most valuable aid in accomplishing the national regeneration of their native land. Strong in numbers, influential in position, gifted with high intelligence and clear political sagacity, and withal intensely national, there is today an Irish power in England which, if marshalled and led with one desire and one aim, would make the possession of power by any political party inimical to Irish interests or Irish rights an utter impossibility. Practically the urban constituencies are at their disposal, and hence, if so minded, the power of what is known as the great Liberal party is in their hands. In London this power is probably greater than elsewhere, save in Liverpool. In some of the suburban constituencies, such as Southwark, it is paramount. An Irish middle class, which, though limited in numbers, has intelligence and influence, backed by the great army of Irish industry which swarms in the marts and the docks, and whose voice is potent in the democratic council or popular assembly, if combined and led, could be made a power of such importance in London as to practically direct the politics of the very centre of English life and action. The patriotism, the will, the power exists – organisation alone is wanting. There are Home Rule Associations and Irish political and literary unions of much promise existing in London, but none whose scope embraces the whole, or whose work could unaided produce the results which the means at the disposal of the Irish people places within their power. The destiny of our country was never more manifestly in the hands of the people than at the present moment, and this is as true of the Irish in England as of their brethren at home – but in England, as in Ireland, the one thing required is Union. Without this, effort is fruitless – with it, all can be accomplished.

On this point I shall have something further to say in a future letter. Details of the moral, social, religious and political state of the Irish in London, as well as of the influence they exercise on the thought and sentiment of the English people, must also be reserved for a future occasion.

Letter II

London, July 8, 1872

Last week I briefly glanced at the extremes of Irish society in London, noted the prodigality with which Irish wealth is squandered in the aristocratic haunts of Belgravia, in the precincts of the Parks, and the purliens of the Haymarket, and cursorily pointed to the squalid misery and degradation of the poor East-end outcasts, as the victims of the vicious system which promotes the expatriation of the Irish people to become the hardest of toilers and severest of strugglers here, and in too many instances to sink to the lowest level of human degradation, to the utter destruction of their bodies and the ruin of their souls. To this subject I shall have again to revert. There is a tale to be told – a picture to be painted – shocking to the eyes, the ears, the hearts of Irishmen – a picture from which, did I consult my own feeling, I should turn in loathing, and neither see nor paint it. But if I obeyed the instinct which prompts this feeling, I should be but half performing the task which your Commission has confided to me. I should be but presenting the sunny side of the picture, and passing over the dark and dismal vales and chasms where crouches the prowling tiger and coils the venomous and deadly serpent, with the fire of the demon in his eyes and the virus of hell in his fangs. I should be showing the gain without indicating the loss, misleading instead of leading, favouring the growth of darkness where of all places on earth light is most needed, indirectly aiding the curse and crime of English misrule in Ireland by omitting to call down condemnation on one of the fellest and foulest of its results. I should not, in fact, be fulfilling my Commission if I omitted anything in describing the condition of our people in this country which would tend to produce a false impression and represent them in any state but that in which they really exist. This I mean to do with the strictest adherence to fact. I shall give the result of inquiry and experience, and trace to their true causes the dreadful effects which I have witnessed or have gleaned from others of unquestioned authority and experience, leaving the responsibility to rest on those who are mainly, if not wholly, accountable for the wreck and ruin which pursues too many of the Irish people in the towns of Great Britain. Whatever be the effect, my conscience will be free from the charge of having witnessed in silence the destruction of our people in England, and thus so far assist in screening the real authors of the woe and misery which I have seen, and in abetting the iniquitous rule which has caused and continues to perpetuate the evil.

But first I shall review the political, social and religious condition of that class of my fellow-countrymen and women who I am proud to say constitute the vast majority of the London Irish – a class that reflects the highest honour and credit on the patriotism and truth, the intellect and the manhood, the integrity and purity, of the Irish people – namely, those whose intellect is the source of their income – those who have manfully toiled from the ranks to independent middle-class positions – those who are in the ranks of skilled labour and manual arts requiring the education of brain and hand – and the strong and mighty mass of our honest, hard-working fellow-countrymen who from year to year win their daily bread by the lowest and severest manual occupations. These classes combined constitute an Irish power in London which in point of intellect, patriotic earnestness, energetic manhood, and fidelity to faith and fatherland, are not excelled by any section of the Irish people on earth. But there are many things in London which tend to limit the effects which one would naturally be led to expect from such a force; and hence results up to the present have not answered the expectations of those who have imposed on themselves the patriotic task of combining the whole force of the Irish people in London with the view of effectual joint political action. The chief of these is that the Irish people are scattered through nearly every district of London, or dotted here and there in the vast human wilderness, almost as effectually separated as if each was an Irish colony in some large and unexplored empire. Here the difficulty [is] of bringing the people together for joint intellectual or political action. But in each district where Irishmen are to be found, Irish political feeling is instinct, and Irish patriotic feeling stirs the hearts of the people with a thrill as high and as holy as if they had never left their homes in the pleasant dells or the sunny slopes of the "green hills of holy Ireland". Let the rights of Ireland be infringed, or the faith of Ireland slandered or alighted, and the flash of the eye and the flush of the cheek at once shows that no change of time or place alters the faith and fortitude of the Irish heart. The peasant transplanted from the bright and verdant borders of the rivers of Ireland to the muddy waters and smoke-canopied streets of London, brings the brightness and verdure, the love and the faith of his native land in his heart, and under all trials and in all circumstances preserves these precious jewels in his heart of hearts. In toil and difficulty, in weal or woe, in joy or sorrow, these things are the bright spots in the waste of his memory. You may change his lot, but you cannot change his heart; and adversity, which destroys the higher feelings in other races, but increases and intensifies them in him. That holy family affection, which exists in no place in the world in the same degree as in Ireland, is as marked in London as in Limerick. That high intuitive spiritual perception, which is at the same time the cause and support of the faith of Ireland, is as keen and as constant here as at home. The individuality which from the first has been a marked characteristic of the Irish race is nowhere more marked than here. That high moral excellence which, after her faith, is the brightest gem in the casket of Irish virtues has preserved with marvellous power the purity of the Irish people in England, though surrounded by the worst and most degrading influences. The patriotic spirit which has defied the persecution, the fraud and force of ages, and which today burns with an intensity as firm and faithful as at first, is in no place more earnest and intense than here, where every pulse throb of English political and social life has its source and centre. We see all the Irish virtues here, and, all things considered, an amazingly small proportion of the vices peculiar to England – but still a percentage shocking to contemplate and dreadful in its effect. We have the manhood, the faith, the spirit, the purity, the patriotism of Ireland here – only awaiting the time and the hand to organise the whole, incite it to action, and direct its power – and there are not wanting signs, hopeful and assuring, that ere long this good work will be in process of perfection. Already the labour has commenced, and patriotic and intellectual associations have sprung up having in their inception and design all the purpose and promise of success. Unity and action are yet required to make the whole an effective force. But clear heads and resolute wills are not wanting to effect this; and I have every confidence that within a very short time the Irish people of London will present a front so strong and compact to the enemies of Irish rights as to astonish the statesmen who fancy that, at least in London, they have all the power in their own hands – and bring encouragement and hope to the brave and true in Ireland, who, through good and evil report, have devoted toil and thought to Ireland, till at last the spirit of the people has been roused to action, and the nation proclaims she must have restored to her the full measure of her rights.

If we could mass together the sum of Irish intellect in London, the aggregate would surprise and pain the Irishman who contemplates the uses to which, almost as a necessary consequence of our dependence, it must be applied. It dominates in the studios, shines in the closet, and educates and rules in the press. It is found on the platform and in the pulpit, in the schools and on the press. The highest plastic and sculptural art is Irish. The genius that directs the first of pictorial magazines – the *Art Journal* – is Irish. The designs of many of the highest pictorial illustrations produced in London are Irish. The mind that conceived her latest great public building was Irish; and the living representative of that mind is still the highest man of his profession. The latest public work of art produced in London – the Prince Albert Memorial – would be simply hideous were not the deformity of the design relieved by the chaste and beautiful conceptions of two Irish sculptors.[1] In truth, the mark of Irish genius is stamped on English in almost every department, in every instance conferring grace and spiritual beauty on all its touches.

In the literary world, whether in book, magazine, or

newspaper, Irish genius furnishes a large percentage of what is brighest and best. If the novel presents original portraiture of character, and the dialogue is pure and brilliant, a glance at the title-page reveals the Hibernian paternity of the author. The magazine article is light, graceful, and sparkling, or the review profound, logical, and erudite; and you think, who may have furnished the sparkling humour in the one case, or the learning that speaks of thought and toil in the other? It is, in every second or third instance, an Irishman who furnishes the matter which challenges your inquiry. From the days of Congreve, Steele, and Goldsmith, to those of Maxwell, Lover, and Lever, the brightest as well as the purest of the magazine and serial literature of London has been supplied by Irishmen [as well]. The Irish names who have figured in the first rank are too well known to need recapitulation; but in the lower and intermediate ranks the proportion of Irish writers on the London press is an unknown mystery outside the ranks of the initiated.[2] There is not a newspaper in London without its one, two, three, and four Irish writers and Irish reporters on its staff – indeed, Irish reporters are not alone numerous, but are the best and the ablest who supply the daily papers with the Court and Parliamentary records of the day. In the Gallery of the House of Commons, the faces longest familiar to the habitues of the place – the names that stand highest for accuracy and facility – are Irish. Such names as Doyle, Hanly, Kearnin, Murphy, O'Halloran, and Daly are but types of a class both able and numerous. In the next higher grade – that of sub-editors – the Irish element largely prevails. Among the leader writers and reviewers Irishmen more than hold their own – in the former case, in too many instances, as the mere mercenaries of the English interest – prepared to turn, metaphorically, on the spit their own kith and kin, at an hour's notice at the usual stipulated prices of two or three guineas an article. But there are other Irish writers who, though compelled to labour for the intellectual aggrandisement of England, scorn the mercenary work of the mere hireling, and preserve the honour of their country and the whiteness of their souls. The highest as well as the fairest of English political organs has more than one Irish contributor of high order and strict integrity. The ablest and most inveterate of the Radical journals has its keenest and most caustic article written weekly by an Irishman. These are the political extremes, but in all the intermediate degrees the case is similar. From the deep baritone of the *Thunderer* to the puny piping of the *Clerkenwell News*, Irish brains and Irish breath supply the inspiration and the harmony. Take away the Irish intelligence from the daily and hebdomadal press of London, and the world would wonder what a curse of stupidity, what a blight of dullness had fallen on the intellect of England. That man who so haughtily lectures foreign Powers (I mean weak ones) is an Irishman. So, I am afraid, is he who supplies that semi-supplicating whine which is sent forth when England is desirous of evading the responsibility of her acts, or wishes to placate the great man at the head of affairs in a nation which is powerful and menacing. It is the same with the magazines. Till the other day, when the pen dropped from the lifeless hand of Lever, the most pleasing sarcasm, couched in the most sparkling humour which English magazine literature has seen for quarter of a century, appeared above the well-known *non be plume* of "Cornelius O'Dowd". The ablest papers in politico-social and international questions are from the pens of Irishmen. So is that pretty and pleasing storiette over which Miss sighs in the latest issue of the Penny Sensationalist. Everywhere – above, below, in the mean, and at the extremes – the intellect of Ireland is supplying mental food for England precisely in the same manner and for the same reason that the Irish farmer caters to the animal wants of John Bull. There is no scope for their talents at home, because their country is a beggared province, with its heart withering at home while its intellect is wandering abroad in vague but uncertain pursuit of the fame for which it yearns. Oh! how glorious would be her destiny if the mighty wealth of intellect with which she has dowered other lands – even that of her enemy – were devoted to her own glory and devoted to her own service.

Next week I shall have something to say about the Irish Home Rule organisations established by our countrymen in this great city; the work they have done and the work they propose to do.

Letter III

London, July 16, 1872

So much for the mental tribute which Ireland pays to England as one of the consequences of her degrading dependency. But there is another working and acting Irish intellectual life apart from this which is pregnant with promise for the future – an intellectual life which is active, far-seeing, and disciplined in political thought, and proudly and intensely devoted to Ireland. This life is wholly, or partly free from literature. You sometimes encounter it on the press – but oftener meet it in the haunts and resorts of trades – and oftenest in the streets and in the workshops – 'mid the builders and the wharfingers. In this, the thinking and toiling mass of Irish in London, and in the class which has worked its way from toil to middle-class competence, are to be found men of much power, real patriotism, and disciplined capacity for political action. Were it not that it would seem invidious, I could point to names whose possessors have all the attributes of thinkers and statesmen; and behind these, hundreds of others who are endeavouring, by education and training, to train themselves for effective service in the struggle for independence on which we are entering. From these have sprung up the Home Rule Associations which have multiplied and spread so rapidly within the last few months – and in these are to be found the more eager and earnest nationalists who desire other means of accomplishing the liberation of their country, but restrain their ardour in the hope that this last effort at conciliation may prove a reality. The power of Home Rule in London is great and rapidly progressing. There have been up to the present six branch associations established in the principal Irish centres of the metropolis, and various other sections are in process of organisation. In a few months, in pursuance of a plan and purpose for the creation of new sections, the number of branches will be increased to fifty, and the members to tens of thousands. The existing branches are at Poplar, Whitechapel,

Wapping, Rotherhithe, and Fulham. These branches regularly meet and have already done much to popularise the cause both among the Irish and the English people. Though much has been done, they are only on the threshold of their labours, and their constitution litte more than provisional; but the scheme for the future submitted to me by the president is so well adapted to local circumstances and requirements, and so well calculated to effect the purpose aimed at, that little prescience is required to foresee the success of the movement and its effect on the political status of the Irish people resident in London. Indeed, I think it advisable at the present time, when Irishmen through the various towns in England are forming themselves into branch associations, to submit to them through the *Nation* the plan which promises so well in London.

At present the branch associations are directed by a General Council and an executive of six, with the President. These decide on all matters in relation to the holding of meetings, the formation or acceptance of new branches, and, generally, of all things affecting the progress or action of the entire body. The Council is not limited as to numbers, but to be increased in proportion to the extension of branches till the whole of the Metropolitan districts are included, and, after that, such other branches as may choose to become affiliated to the London Central Association. Each branch will have its own executive locally, and will be represented in the Central Council by representatives elected by ballot and the president and secretary in virtue of their office. When the General Council is established, the Executive is to be elected from the body, and is to possess plenary power during its period of office. All elections in the branches are to be subject to a veto of this Council, and all its orders are to be held binding on all the sections. There is to be a general fund applicable to all the London branches, so that the poorer branches may be aided and supported by the richer. An order of organisers, or rather teachers, are to be appointed, on whom will devolve the duty of delivering addresses or lectures, locally or generally, in order to win over the slow, and promote the formation of branches. All branches and members admitted are to accept unconditionally and without reservation all the rules and regulations and to subscribe to the principles of the London Home Rule Association. Branches outside the metropolis wishing for affiliation to the London Association are to have their own laws, rules, and fiscal arrangements – the object of union being mutual advice and suggestion. No matter how advanced the opinions of individuals, subscription to the principle of Home Rule is all the condition of membership required, but this subscription in every case is to be held indispensable. A foundation for an Irish census and the registration of voters in London and suburbs will be one of the first practical tasks undertaken by the executive and council. The power thus accurately known, trained, and organised is to be used on every occasion when there is an opportunity, and always in furtherance of the object aimed at by the association. In vestry, municipal, and parliamentary elections this force is to be used in furtherance of Irish interests – locally as well as nationally. So large is the Irish population of London, and so great the political power which thus organised will be at the service of the national cause, that a confident opinion prevails that in over half the metropolitan constituencies the Irish vote will either materially influence or entirely control the elections. Already overtures are being made, and candidates whispering of Home Rule. In many of the constituencies the Irish are masters of the situation, and are certain to use the power at their command.

Thus far the London Home Rule Association has proved itself well worthy of the mission on which it has entered. It has extended its own power and is rapidly extending its influence outside even in English thought and opinion – the rich, the poor – the high, the low – the learned, the unlearned, have been more or less induced to recognise the justice of its principles and the practicability of its aims. The recent meeting at the Agricultural Hall did much to promote this end. On the platform were many persons of eminence, both politicians and literary men, representing England, Scotland, and America, all, or nearly all, of whom were agreeably disappointed on finding that Home Rule was not the bugbear they had fancied, and that, instead of promoting revolution, it would lead to the tranquillity and strength of the empire. In one or two instances Englishmen of high intellectual status asked to be admitted as members. Below this class a large section of the democracy of London are favourable to the views of the Home Rulers, and the ablest and most prominent of their leaders acknowledge in its programme the prolation of the policy of the future. This I have heard from them myself, and this I am assured by those who know more about them, is not the opinion of the thoughtful few alone, but of the energetic, impulsive, and progressive many.

Apart from the great body of Irishmen in London who have made literature a profession, there exists, as I before remarked, among the middle class, the artisan and labouring Irish population, a political and intellectual force, strong in numbers, high in mental attainments and ability, and important in its influence, which is gradually extending to ranks and classes outside the circles to which Irish thought and Irish opinion are supposed to be limited. Hitherto this important element in the social and political progress of the Irish in London has been left unknown in the byeways of life, few knowing of its existence and scarcely any effort being made to develop and foster its power. In London, the unattached Irish intellect – if I may so call it – existed as flowers in the wilderness, that bloom, fling their perfume in the air of the desert, and die, leaving no memory of their beauty and fragrance behind them. The man skilled in the literature and lore of his native land, fancying himself alone and lost in this mighty and unsympathetic wilderness of life, knew nothing of his brethren who, like himself, had stored their minds with a knowledge of the language, the records, and antiquities of their native land. The profound antiquarian or ripe Gaelic scholar, who, in addition to the stores of knowledge borne with him from his home in Ireland, had culled from the records of the British Museum the gems of Irish thought and the flowers of Irish intellect which, but for the blight of alien rule, would have fed and adorned the literature of his native land, knew nothing of the kindred spirit who yearned in the heart of the great city for communion with those to whom the language and love of the Old Land were dear. The scattered Gael lived in the stranger's land unknown to each other, unconscious of the light that was hidden in their midst, or of the influence it would exercise when revealed. A few of those who knew their power and appreciated the force of example and union, resolved to remove this unnatural intellectual estrangement, and combine the Gaelic element in the British metropolis with the view of revealing the beauties of its ancient lore and literature – reviving the old language so as to prevent its extinction, and bringing the public acquainted with Celtic history, archaeology, philosophy, philology, and antiquarian remains. The result was the establishment of the Celtic Society of London, which has, since its foundation, little more than six months since, brought together and combined in its members and its management men whose names are a guarantee for ability and energy, zeal and progress.

To define all the aims of this Society would be beyond the scope of a letter such as this. Suffice it to say that it is the only Celtic Association in the English metropolis – that it aims at tracing the memorials "of the glorious old race which, at the dawn of the historic period, ruled the Continent of Europe, peopled Great Britain, and in the present day constitutes a large portion of the inhabitants of England" – that race which, from its intellectual centre in Ireland, from the fifth to the ninth century, "rekindled and preserved throughout Christendom the lights of literature and civilisation", and which in that country has left such rich stories of "early vernacular literature", and such "a large and precious collection of exquisite art in gold, silver and bronze", as to be unique among the artistic antiquities of the period at which they were wrought.

But the Celtic Society of London does not propose to limit its labours to the study, cultivation, and development of Irish literature and antiquities. Its labours are intended to embrace all that appertains to the history, literature, and archaeology of the whole Celtic family. "One in name and in fame are the sea-divided Gaels" might be appropriately taken as its motto. It proposes to explore the libraries of Europe, public and private, where Celtic records or literary remains are known to exist – to prepare and print descriptive catalogues of the various MSS collections – to maintain a professorship of Gaelic and Comparative Philology, and to provide instruction in the Celtic dialects – to promote the objects of the Society by meetings, lectures, &c.; to compile and publish dictionaries in Gaelic and Welsh, and in time "to issue a periodic journal for the publication of the transactions of the Society". The work aimed at is brave and noble; but the spirit in which it is undertaken, and the catholic scope of its objects, commend it not less to the generous appreciation and support of the public than does the purpose of its inquiries to the *literateur* and the archaeologist. This is shown in the desire which it evinces to "investigate to what extent the Celtic element prevailed in Europe – the area over which the various dialects were spoken, and the remains of them which may still be traced", and to enlist in this inquiry and promote social intercourse between the various branches of the Celtic family, whether Irish, Scotch, Welsh, Britons, or French.

Up to the present the chief work of the Society has been devoted to organisation and influencing those to favour its purpose who, from wealth, literary eminence, or social position, can aid in advancing the object of its foundation; and in this, so far, it has been successful. As a recent meeting of its members, in their rooms in Doughty Hall, Bedford-row, Mr. Maguire, M.P., presided, and expressed himself in very high terms in relation to the objects of the Society and the advance it had already made. As might be easily expected, the Society has as yet realised none of the objects for which it has been established; but the Council is engaged in preparing and deciding on works for publication and in making arrangements for extending the ramifications of the Society in other countries. What success may crown an effort so well and worthily begun, it is impossible at present to divine; but the existence of such an Association in the heart of London is a striking proof of the force and energy of Irish genuis, and of the influence it exercises wherever on earth the Irish race have made a home. Perhaps the most striking evidence of this influence is to be found in the fact that though the Society numbers among its members several literary men and persons of many callings and professions, it has originated among the Irish educated artisans and working and middle classes; and that Mr. O'Fallon, the gentleman who conceived the idea of founding such a Society, and to whose zeal in a great measure its present success is due, has no connexion with literature professionally.

That there exists such a Society in London is the best proof of the individuality, aggressive tendency, and absorbing influence of the Irish intellect. That it deserves support, none will deny. That it may receive such support as to place within its power the accomplishment of the ends at which it aims, should be the sincere wish of all lovers of ancient literature, art, and archaeology.

Letter IV

July 23, 1872

I have pointed out the extremes of Irish social life existing in London, and shown that to the system which draws the wealth of Ireland to be squandered in extravagance in the West End is to be attributed the degradation and misery which consume the life and destroy the morals of the Irish people in the East. I have glanced at the intellectual energy shown in the number of Irishmen who swell the ranks of the great literary republic, and the wealth of whose thought has contributed in an eminent degree to the glory and greatness of England – and in doing this have distinguished between the earnest, ardent, honest candidate for the favours of Fame, and the mere mercenary whose sole ambition is circumscribed by the desire to please his paymasters and earn for himself the means of sharing in the flesh-pots of the stranger. I have indicated the worth and power, the grandeur and greatness, of the thinking and toiling masses, in whose ranks are to be found the political force and mental energy out of which have grown the London Home Rule Association and the Celtic Society. There is in all this a conclusive evidence of the splendour and influence of Irish mind and Irish manhood when emancipated from the evil agencies which condemn them to lethargy and inaction at home – for that such is the effect of the present order of things in Ireland none will deny. Such is the blighting effect of foreign rule that to burgeon, bloom, and bear fruit worthy of its strength and fervour, the genius of Ireland must be transplanted out of its native habitat. At home it languishes as the forest trees that pine when the upas loads the atmosphere with its poison. Abroad it flourishes as the scriptural vine, blessing the nations with the pure and precious fragrance of its bloom, and also rich and healthful fruit of its maturity. It is a sad and bitter destiny which compels a nation to hoard and dispense the grandest and noblest of its gifts only for the benefit of aliens and enemies; and such, under the deadly blight of foreign domination, is the destiny of Ireland.

But there is another aspect of Irish life in England – and more particularly in London – which would redound still more to the credit of our expatriated brethren than the nobility of their manhood, the splendour of their intellect, or the constancy and fidelity of their patriotism, if it were not alas! – for the truth must be spoken – that the evil associations of this country have dragged tens, aye, hundreds of thousands of them, down to the lowest depths of temporal misery and eternal ruin. The great body of the people here are pure and pious as they were at home; but the loss, as I before intimated, is fearful to contemplate. In speaking thus, I wish it to be understood that I am not alluding merely to the metropolis, but to England generally, for this letter is not written in London. As I proceed through the different districts where the Irish element largely prevails, I shall be careful to show our strength and indicate our loss. For the present, I must confine myself to London.

Here the evidence of the purity, piety, and fervour of the Irish heart and mind confront one at every turn; and here, too, are evidences of ruin and wretchedness that pain the soul and sicken the heart. The churches that have sprung and are still springing up in all parts of London and its vicinity – indeed, throughout England generally – are examples of the pious generosity of the Irish people. With very rare exceptions, the pence of the poor, not the pounds of the rich, have swelled the funds required for their erection. The people who but a few years since were flung helpless and broken on the shores of the world – like ocean drift after the fury of the storm – have borne with them, wherever they have found a resting-place, the high spiritual and moral attributes which from the first have peculiarly distinguished the race and the nation. I do not entirely rely on my own experience and inquiries in making this statement. So wrote Dr. Todd, the English Catholic priest, in his generous and appreciative papers written in the *Dublin Review* some years ago, and since reprinted.[3] So wrote Mr. Mayhew, when describing the poor in his careful and elaborate work, *The Great World of London*.[4] The Catholic priest testifies to the high spiritual excellence of the Irish in London –

both testify to their immeasurably superior moral condition. "It can be shown", writes Dr. Todd, "by the most indisputable testimony that there is a remarkable difference between" the Irish and the English poor, "so far as religion and morals are concerned. The faith of the Irish is proverbial, and it is really marvellous." In migrating to England, he says, they carry this one treasure, "more precious than rubies", along with them. It is, indeed, in the majority of instances, their all. "Of the Irish in England, as at home," he adds, "it may be asserted with perfect truth that they 'live by the faith'." "They are in a peculiar and striking way a super-natural people. They never lose sight of the unseen world . . . The Invisible is inseparably mixed up with their modes of speech as well as with their habits of thought." "An angel from heaven," he writes, "would find himself much out of place in the costly mansions of Belgrave and Grosvenor Squares." "But let him leave behind him all the grandeur and magnificence of the aristocratic halls of Belgravia, and pass to the crowded dens of the mere Irish . . . and the companion of the Most High would find himself at home." The Irishman's respect for the sacerdotal character he points out as something superior to theological perception, and incidentally explains, in a manner that is almost suggestive, the Irishman's preference for the priests of his own country – a preference in too many instances disregarded, and in some superciliously overborne by those unacquainted with the mysteries of the Irish mind and heart.

Of the exaltation of the Irish mind and heart in all that appertains to matters of faith, Dr. Todd speaks in the highest terms. "Many a little saint now in heaven", he says, "owes its salvation to some poor Irish servant who procured for it the blessing which its own parents despised or neglected." Indeed, the burden of all he says is that the highest spiritual perception is inherent in the Irish nature, and superior to all the knowledge of the most excited theosophists. A higher authority still – indeed, the highest in the Church of England – a prelate whose heart is as large as his piety and learning are eminent, and his life pure and self-sacrificing – in a conversation with the writer of these letters some months since, testified in still higher terms to the spiritual exaltation and moral superiority of the Irish people. "If there is a spot on earth", were his words, as near as I can remember them, "where the faith exists in its primitive simplicity, purity, and fervour, it is in your country; and how your poor people preserve their faith and their morals, exposed as they are here to all sorts of trials and temptations, except in the providence of God, is a marvel. No other people would pass through the ordeal with so little loss." This is, indeed, high testimony. Would to Heaven it were as true universally as it presents itself to the mind of the good and great Archbishop of Westminster![5]

But it is not alone the virtue of Faith, with its attendant morality, which the Irish bear with them and preserve in England. The generous and expansive charity which has ever been a trait in the national character, is as evident by the Thames and the Tyne and the Mersey, as by the Liffey, the Shannon, the Barrow, and the Blackwater. They are charitable to their own, charitable to strangers – charitable in all that concerns temporal matters – prodigally so when the claim is made in the name of religion. "The Catholic poor of Ireland are without question", writes Dr. Todd, "pre-eminent for their charity and benevolence to one another." They give and lend to each other anything and everything they possess, and will "deprive themselves of absolute necessities of food and raiment that they may help a sick parent or assist a more needy neighbour". To the Church they give largely and liberally. "Take away", said a good, zealous, generous, English priest to your correspondent some years since, "your people, and we would soon have few churches left and very little to support them." So, too, says Dr. Todd: "From their scanty and precarious earnings they give largely and liberally to the service of religion. They support our priests and build our churches. Speaking relatively, they give far more than the rich in retributions for masses and in other acts of alms-giving." He cites Father Kelly, whose church on the Commercial-Road is almost, if not wholly, supported by the Irish people, and says that, with a few trifling exceptions, the expenses of building his church and appurtenances "have been paid by the pence of the poor"; and the priest of Alderney (who would imagine an Irish population in

Alderney?), who says that "though there are 500 French Catholics in his mission, they contribute nothing to the Church. He is supported entirely by the Irish poor". Almost on the coast of France an Irish population supports a mission of which the French inhabitants of the island derive equal advantages. In what other race on earth would such fervour and charity be found?

Not alone the kindliness and charity peculiar to the Irish nature are to be found here. Whatever gave life – in its joy and gladness, its gloom and sorrow – a charm at home is here to soothe the lonelier sorrow of the exile's lot, or harmonise with the varying emotions inseparable from a destiny such as his. The songs of his youth ("Old songs of our Land," that bring back memories of the heroism and struggles of the past, incite to hope and promise in the future, or stir to tenderer emotions the affection and purity of the Irish heart) – cheer the weary toiler through the day, or bear to his home in the dingy and crowded alley, when the day's labour is over and the twilight thickens the city's heavy gloom, the memory and light of the bright homestead in Ireland when first he heard them chanted by sister or friend, mother or lover. The weary spirit is cheered even in the saddest and loneliest of Irish homes – the lorn heart forgets its pain, and the dimmed eye is relumed with its olden light, as the melody of the past sweeps over the soul, and the memories of long ago arise beneath its spell and people the fancy with the forms of the distant and the departed. It is an illusion that rises but to vanish, but it charms the spirit for the moment, and is in harmony with the emotions of his kindred over the earth. Like an angel with a message from home, the spirit of melody and song enters and sits by the hearth of the Irish exile, bearing on its wings the light and glory, the passion and joy, of the dear old land. Oh, what a joy and a gladness have this gift of melody and song been to the Irish people. From the day when Columbkille, by the stormy waters of Iona, soothed his sad soul to the strains of the clairseach, whose strings poured forth their wealth of melody to his master touch, and on through the long and dreary penal period down to this our own day, when the ancient musical glory of Ireland is represented in the solitary airs of the blind fiddler or piper, who has followed the fortunes of the inhabitants of his native village into the uncongenial atmosphere of the English towns, what a blessing and a boon have our music and our melodies been to the persecuted and despised Irish race! Here the old airs are played with all their hidden graces and all their interpolated errors. Here the old songs are sung with all their fire and pathos, grace and beauty. Here, too, are heard to ring the spirit-stirring strains of our time – whose very energy is a power that creates the conditions to make the prophecy of the future a reality. We have in England, in fact, a full epitome of Irish life. Inveterate in its individuality, the Irish heart bears with it wherever it goes all that it loved and cherished at home, and so preserves the treasures of antiquity as in a casket, enwreathed with the freshest and fairest of the flowers of youth. "The stranger has heard her lament on his plains", but her song is no longer the song of sorrow. There is hope, and trust, and defiance in its tone. The very songs chanted in the heart of England have changed, save on the lips of the old, from the "sigh of sadness" to the proud paean of patriotism. Across the Atlantic we hear the old melodies set to lyrics of hope and daring, and in imagination listen to the thunder of Irish eloquence rising above the swell of the ocean surges. In England, as in America, there are forces working in the very inner life of the people which cannot fail to influence materially our grand movement for national regeneration.

Letter IV (continued) *July 23, 1872*

The singular purity of the Irish heart, which, next to the fidelity with which it has clung to the olden faith, is the proudest boast of the Irish people, if not so signally marked here as at home, is nevertheless immeasurably superior to that of the people among whom our people are forced to reside. Go where you may, ask whom you will, and the reply is the same. There is no comparison between the morality of the Irish and English people in the same class, or indeed in any class, in the English towns. "When we have made a full and fair deduction for those cases of scandal and sin which do really exist among them," says Dr. Todd, "the genuine and sincere purity of the Irish people will still be the most remarkable feature in their character. Purity is the rule; impurity the exception. There are certain kinds of sin which are almost wholly unknown among them." And Mr. Mayhew, in the work before mentioned, while testifying in the highest terms to the religious zeal of the Irish in London, pays under the circumstances the very highest tribute to the singular purity of the poorest and most hardworking Irish female population – the London street sellers. They keep, he says, distinct from the English street sellers, and for the sake of all that is good and pure, it is well they should. With these latter, he adds, "religion is almost a nonentity", and their morals are still worse. "The Irish women", he says, "present two characteristics which distinguish them from the London coster-woman generally – they are chaste, and, unlike the 'coster girls', very seldom form any connexion without the sanction of the marriage tie." "They may," he continues, "pay less regard to truth, but they unquestionably pay a greater regard to chastity. They are, moreover, attentive to religious observances." The Irish girls who are street sellers are generally the daughters of persons engaged in the same calling. "They grow up", says Mr. Mayhew, "in street selling, and as they rarely form impure connexions, and as no one may be induced to offer them marriage, their life is often one of strict celibacy." Here we have the testimony of the English priest corroborated by the Protestant English gentleman. What higher testimony could be adduced of the strength and purity of the Irish heart? They live in an atmosphere reeking with sin. Their daily companions – almost associates, for they cannot always shun them – are amongst the lowest and most degraded of the English poor, without religion, without morals, festering in vices the very mention of which is shocking to human nature. From this lazar house of iniquity, like the vapours of Phlegethon, ascends the pestiferous stream of immorality which creeps into the veins, poisoning all with which it comes in contact. There is a perpetual epidemic of vice in London. Irish virtue is the only prophylactic which resists it. The pure Irish blood flings off the miasma, and is untainted by the poison, save in exceptional cases to be hereafter mentioned. As I write, the *Daily Telegraph* lies before me, containing an article in its usual stilted style, exulting at the prospect of the passing of a

Bastardy Act, intended as a bribe to mothers not to murder their illegitimate offspring. It is only, it appears, by paying a higher tribute to vice that infanticide is to be checked in England. And it is in such a country, and surrounded by such influences, that Irish virtue and Irish purity are to be preserved. That it is preserved in so remarkable a degree is marvel. That thousands – nay, tens and hundreds of thousands – of our poor people should contract the contagion of vice and rot in moral leprosy like the rest, is no marvel at all. Only a person well acquainted with London and the other larger towns of England can form any idea of how they are tempted, and what they have to endure. An angel from Heaven could scarcely pass through the same dread ordeal, and preserve its glory undimmed and its pinions untarnished.

But now we must turn and view the other side of the picture. We have seen the force and strength of Irish patriotism in London, marked the thinker and toiler working hand in hand for Ireland – beheld the marvellous force and aggressive tendency of Irish intellect – struggling arduously to attain the highest places in literature, art, and science – seizing the most exalted positions, and maintaining its right to have and to hold the foremost places in the front rank. We have seen the fervent, zealous piety – the ardent charity – ther heroic fidelity – the wonderful strength and purity of the Irish heart. But we have not seen all. There are dark and dread caverns hidden in the landscape of light which must be explored, and the wretched sojourners in their dismal depths exhumed and revealed. Alas, that it should be so – but so it is. There are thousands – tens of thousands of the Irish people in London alone who are lost – lost irretrievably. There is no gainsaying it, and to shut one's eyes to it and see only the good, without estimating the evil and the loss, would be the merest criminal folly. Our people are crushed, physically debased, and morally ruined by the dread circumstances almost inseparable from their lot. The poverty which drove them from home is their evil genius abroad. Their own improvidence – it is only fair to add – in some instances lead to their degradation and destruction. The drink demon is the fatal phantom that lures thousands to their doom. Drink – drink is the crime and the curse of Irishmen in this country. It is the stigma which, of all others, is the most fatal to their character, the cloud that hides the brilliant lustre of their many virtues. But for this the lightness of the calendar of Irish crime in England would be as exceptionally remarkable as it is in Ireland. But without considering this, and entirely apart from the evil and the loss which it entails, the condition of the Irish people in England, and particularly in the large cities, is such that it cannot be contemplated in all its relations, and leave a doubt that dreadful ruin to faith and morals must result from the associations surrounding them. They come here poor. They have to herd as a consequence among the poorest and most degraded of the English masses. Their immediate neighbours are of the "criminal" classes. The language of vice is the vernacular of their neighbourhood. the crimes they abhorred at home are incidents in the everyday life of those among whom they are forced to live. That:

> Monster of such frightful mein,
> That to be hated, needs but to be seen.[6]

loses half its dread terrors by familiarity. The associations, particularly for the young, are most pernicious. The children grow up breathing an atmosphere of impurity from the first, by which their whole moral nature is vitiated. The young girl fresh from Ireland is forced, from her poverty, on arrival into positions most detrimental to her safety. The lower middle-class, the small shopkeepers – often devoid of religion and morals – or the still lower and more demoralised Jews of Spitalfields and Whitechapel, are the chief employers of the unsophisticated Irish girl when she first arrives in London. She is strong and willing, goes for low wages, and not over fastidious in matters of food and accommodation, and hence she becomes the prey of the mercenary and immoral classes I have pointed out. In multitudes of cases the end is as might be anticipated. The virtuous Irish girl is ruined. She is degraded in her own estimation, and sinks into lower depths still, till, in the end, the bright and blooming Irish girl who left her native village as pure as the breeze on the heather of her native hills, with the benediction of the old priest who counselled and guided her from childhood on her head, and the fond wishes of generous friends and devoted parents following her in the land of the stranger, sinks broken-hearted and lost beneath the burden of her sin (verily, indeed, more sinned against than sinning), her young spirit sullied and defiled, her young life trampled out in the triumph of vice in its never-ending heartless procession.

I paint no fancy picture. Would to God this were only a fancy creation! It is not. It is a sad and bitter reality, and not in one case alone, but in thousands. Here is an instance which may serve as a type of the many.

I am in Bethnal Green, and the time is the summer twilight. A woman – evidently Irish – with the faint lines of beauty still in her face, and all the easy grace of her race in her carriage, emerges from the doorway of a dingy gin-shop. She is but the merest wreck of what she once must have been. Poverty and vice had tainted her blood and discoloured her skin, till it had grown to a hue between pale green and chocolate. On her arm lay, or rather hung, a child of some two summers, with a wasted form and discoloured skin like its mother's, its listless head and limp limbs depending powerless from the mother's half-sustaining arm. The child's face and the mother's arm were of the same wasted livid hue. I approach and ask a passing question – an inquiry for the nearest way to a certain place. She civilly supplies the information. I make a casual allusion to Ireland, and she turns her head and is silent. I draw her into conversation. An allusion to home and its associations touched the fountain of her feeling, and the worn bosom heaved and the tear glistened in the dimmed eye. An English woman in similar circumstances would meet her interlocutor with a brazen stare and assail his ears with filthy language. The poor, fallen Irish woman simply melted into tears, leant against the wall, and sobbed audibly. It is rarely that the demon entirely displaces the good spirit and takes entire possession of the Irish heart. The poor creature, soothed and softened, hesitated not to tell the story of her early life, her fall, and her misery. She was born in a village in Kerry, and came to England when she was eighteen, found a place through a

Servants' Registry, in the family of an English shopkeeper, where she was ruined and disgraced. Had neither friend nor refuge when flung homeless in the streets; and so sank from bad to worse till reduced to the wreck I saw – wretched, worn, and consumpted, standing trembling on the verge of the grave, which will soon mercifully close over her and hide her shame and her sorrows till the last dread day. I advised her where to go to seek comfort and succour. I hope – if only for the sake of the child – she did as I advised; but I fear not. More probably, the small coin I gave her was expended in the gin-shop, to bring the benediction of forgetfulness to her broken heart. I learned her story afterwards from others. It was in every respect substantially true. Poor thing! she never let her people know where she was from the date of her first fall. She would not pain the mother's heart, or bring sorrow and shame to the grey hairs of the father that loved and cherished her memory. They have probably fancied her dead; they may be dead now; and so she will sink to the grave unknown and forgotten, leaving the little waif of humanity which I saw to live or die. Better it should die. The criminal's fate would probably be its heritage did it survive.

This, reader, is but a case in thousands. There are some half a million of Irish by birth and blood in London, and among them – notwithstanding the superior spiritual gifts and virtue of our race – the percentage of the fallen is fearful. That bright-eyed boy whom you meet in the street, and whose mirth and humour, despite his "looped and windowed raggedness", commend him to the notice of the casual observer, is the son of Irish parents, graduating in the streets for the profession of a criminal. That fair girl you see rolling in the dust, who, though ragged and dirty, has the seraph's light in her eyes, must be brought up amid sights and sounds which render the preservation of her purity impossible. They breathe moral pestilence, and it poisons their blood. They follow evil example, and sink to utter and hopeless ruin.

I am aware that all possible is being done to check this terrible moral canker that preys so horribly on our poor people. I know the Archbishop and his clergy labour with untiring zeal to arrest its growth and mitigate its evils. The Archbishop is himself essentially the pastor of the children and the poor. For those he thinks, for those he labours. But the life of prelate and priest in London is one continuous struggle with a demon whose name is Legion. All that can be done they do; but nothing short of Divine interposition can arrest the dread evil. The Archbishop still needs thirty-one schools for the poor children of his archdiocese. This number represents accommodation for at least 5,000 children, who, we may infer, are in their absence without the means of instruction. This alone shows the difficulty of the situation. But this is only one item in the account from which the moral and spiritual loss of the Irish people are to be estimated.

An interview with Dr. Todd at Greenwich confirmed me in the high estimate I had formed, from reading his pamphlet, of the moral grandeur and spiritual superiority of the Irish people in England. That they are immeasurably superior to any other people in the metropolis is an undisputed fact, in support of which he has given me authority to use his name. When asked, if since he wrote his pamphlet he saw any reason to alter a word of his judgment, his reply was "certainly not, but the contrary". In such a centre of vice the Irish are pure to a marvel, but the standard of purity has to be judged by comparison with a people who hardly know moral restraint, and though relatively very high, there is still a dreadful loss. The cure for all this is to keep the people at home, and this can only be done by a radical alteration of the relations existing between Ireland and England. The Irish people in England, as a consequence of the present system, are destroyed in more ways than one. The strength of our manhood is crushed and worn out in the worst and most wasting labour here – labour that in the majority of cases breaks down man's strength and vigour in four or five years; whilst the land which nature designed as the heritage of our race is converted into profitless waste by the very system whose operation drives the people here. It is the same system that converts into social outcasts the good and virtuous daughters of Ireland, who under a different *regime* would be the happy mothers of pious and loving children at home. The system, however we look on it, is a curse. It wastes our wealth and resources, degrades our manhood, and destroys the purity of our womanhood who have the misfortune to be forced to seek a living in England. The extent to which this is done may be inferred when I add that at the very least one in ten of the Irish in London and their offspring – both men and women – are lost to morals and to faith; and the percentage is still higher in some of the other towns in England, as I shall hereafter have occasion to point out. This, according to the most accurate estimate which I have been enabled to make, would leave some 40,000 for London alone, and from three to four hundred thousand Irish souls lost throughout Great Britain – a dread holocaust to offer up for the re-Christianisation of the English people.

But how is this to be arrested? Ask the Irish priest, and he will tell you – "Keep the people at home". From London to Newcastle this is the suggestive advice. In the heart of London the Irish priest counsels it. It is so in the Midlands. Farther North, in Yorkshire, the good Fathers of St. Vincent, whose zeal and charity for the Irish poor are worthy of all praise, echo the cry, and add – "It were better they had perished in the famine than come to lose their souls here". They live to suffer – the famine-slain are at rest and happy. One goes North and West but to hear the cry repeated – "Keep the people at home". But how? This is the question; and here arises the responsibility – a fearful and terrible responsibility – whoever is to be held accountable for it. The Irish people leave their homes; and the priests, who knew and trusted to their virtues, know not of their doom. Did they see what I have seen – did they know what Irish priests labouring in English missions well know – with bleeding hearts they would acknowledge that the system which forces them into exile is the deadly curse of our people, and labour with martyr zeal to overthrow it. Whoever comes here, and sees and judges for himself, must go home convinced that he who aids and abets English rule in Ireland is, consciously or unconsciously, not alone guilty of the blood, but of the very souls, of the banished Irish people. Let me not be told the fault is their own. The fault is to those who support the system which drives them from the shores of their own holy and virtuous island into the very hotbeds of infamy in the English towns. People of Ireland – Priests of Ireland

– Prelates of Ireland – ponder this; and weigh well the responsibility of apathy and inaction. Till minute inquiry convinced me of the fact, I never imagined that behind the glorious revelation of Irish virtue in England was this terrible background of misery and loss. That it is so, admits not of the slightest doubt; and on us, one and all, devolves the duty of reversing the policy which has produced it. I expose the evil and point to its cause – not to condemn our poor people, but with the desire to save those who are yet at home. For the sake of Ireland's fair fame – for God's sake – I ask the nation, one and all, to denounce the system and save the people.

Letter V

30th July, 1872

South and west of London there are but few places where the Irish people have permanently located themselves, and in these few not in any considerable numbers. Southwards to Southampton and Portsmouth; south-west, to Plymouth; and westwards, to Bristol – except during the seasons of hay-making and harvest – there are few Irishmen to be met with. Even in the southern towns just mentioned, the Irish population is comparatively limited – not a fifth in proportion to the numbers to be found in towns of equal population in the centre and north of England. Of the numbers scattered among the farmsteads of the southern counties, I can form no estimate. That they are considerable, there is good reason to believe. This is seen whenever a Catholic mission is founded here, as elsewhere in England. At the call of the Church an Irish congregation springs up almost as sudden as the warriors to the bugle of Roderic Dhu. Where they have been hidden no one knows, but the mission is no sooner founded than in flock the Irish, and the temporary house of worship has at once the bulk of its congregation and the nucleus of its support. The nomadic groups that scour the country in the haymaking and harvest season, like birds of passage, leave stragglers behind. These, if they do not become permanent residents, winter occasionally in certain localities, and from these the supporters of new missions are chiefly recruited. In Kent, Sussex, Essex, and Dorset these semi-nomadic Irish are chiefly to be seen, notably in Kent, where in the hop-picking season thousands of the Irish population of London join their brethren from Ireland and elsewhere, and spend a few weeks almost as joyously as the merry grape gatherers of the Continent. Throughout England, indeed, from the end of May to the end of October, groups of Irish are to be met with, chiefly men. They are haymakers and harvesters. The hop-pickers are frequently females. Of these, and of what they have to endure, it is enough to say that the evil influences to which they are exposed are worse than in the worst of the towns. When they can keep together and preserve a sort of family union, all goes comparatively well, but this is seldom the case. Broken into smaller groups, they have to associate with the refuse of the English towns who go out for the season, and the result is what might be anticipated. What was true of the Jews when they entered the Promised Land is true of the poor Irish resident in England today, and truest of all of those who are out hop-picking. The friendship of "the people of the land" is more dangerous to them than their enmity. Their example is evil, their contagion moral ruin. I am not stating this of the English people generally, though on the whole their example is bad enough. I am referring to those with whom the poor Irish are forced to associate, and of those it may be safely affirmed that Christendom does not produce anything lower or worse. Need it be wondered, then, if moral and social ruin is often the consequence of these associations, and that to the dread demon of circumstance the good, the pure, and pious Irish heart is sacrificed? The evil genius that forces the people from their own land drives them here to their ruin in this. To know the extent to which this is done it needs to be seen. I could not describe it in your columns. No people on earth but the Irish would pass through the fiery furnace of iniquity with so little loss. But here, as in London, there is loss – loss great and palpable – trying and terrible. Those who see but the surface know it not. But the canker worm is at the heart of the rose of Irish virtue, and we know its ravages by observing the sweet and glowing leaflets that are blighted and fall but to be trampled in the ruin. The clime in which it bloomed without tarnish – the air that fostered and nourished its beauty – is not in England.

North and north-east from London, till we come to the midlands, except in one or two places in Norfolk, there is little of a resident Irish population; but the class of agricultural labourers is to be found interspersed here as in the south – indeed, here Irish labourers are more numerous – and here possibly the contrast of race is more marked than in any part of England. Here you meet the Celt, with his lithe and agile figure, bright countenance, and indomitable humour, side by side with the slow, inanimate, spiritless Saxon, almost in the same mental and moral condition as when most degraded by the tyranny of his Norman masters. You have evidence here of the undying energy of the Celt, and of the slower and more easily debased nature of the Saxon. The one is square-shouldered and lithe in build and limb, with every fibre of his body instinct with life and strung for action. His eye, dark or grey, is full of light and mirth; and humour is depicted in every lineament of his countenance. His face is mobile and expressive of every passing emotion, revealing his generous feeling and genial nature, as the sunshine does the lights and shades of the summer woods. He lightens his labour by jest and song, and alternately teases and pleases his slow but not ill-natured fellow-workman of the rival race, who is too dull to understand the point of his jokes, but cannot fail to be pleased by his good humour – except, indeed, that he is insulted or provoked too far; and then, indeed, he shows that his humour is but sparkles from the fire that burns within, and which it is dangerous to excite to flame. Touch his faith or his patriotism, and this is seen at once. His good humour tolerates anything short of slighting or sneering at them; but touch either, and his spirit, that was as gentle as the summer breeze on his native heather, becomes as the fury of the hurricane. "His blood is hot, his blow is strong" in a moment, and the aggressor feels the fury and strength of both. Nearly all the disputes ending in riots between English and Irish workmen, of which we so frequently hear, arise from causes such as those.

The typical Saxon found here is a very different being from the Celt. He is slow, heavy, and inelastic, with long back, broad hips, thick and short legs, short neck, pumpkin head, listless, unmeaning eyes, broad, heavy chin, and mouth a straight line across the face. His hair and skin are usually a light straw colour; with scarcely a shade to distinguish them. His beard, in common with all inferior races, is scant and weak. He bears his body about with a slow, rolling motion, and is averse to athletic exercises. His body tends to obesity, or, if not well nourished, becomes pale and flabby. His countenance is the index of his mind, which is slow, dull, and unimaginative – not capable of originality or the less elevated mental qualities which favour acquirement and incline to study. His ideas are limited to his daily wants – his language the merest jargon. This is a picture of the typical Saxon, as found in his primitive state in the agricultural districts of England; but it would by no means apply to the typical Englishman, who is scarcely more Saxon than he is Roman, and is more Celtic than either. But these are the associates of the Irish agricultural labourer; and as they are no better morally than physically or mentally, there can be little but evil to be drawn from the contact.

But the strength and power of the Irish populace in England is to be found in the strongholds of English energy and industry in the midlands and the north; and here I purpose next week to follow in their footsteps and mark their power and progress, noting, at the same time, the wreck and the loss that are everywhere apparent. The good and the brilliant qualities of our race are everywhere to be seen; but alas! there is evil to chronicle, and ruin that must be pointed out. But, if I note the sore, I shall not fail to indicate the cause and remedy.

North of London, on the east, there is a sparse and sporadic Irish population, but in no place showing evidence of the life, force, and intelligence to be found in the Midlands and the North till we come to Lincoln and Leicestershire. On the West, till Bristol is reached, there is very little evidence of an Irish population. The Irish here are dispersed through the farmsteads, and are occasionally to be seen in the villages and towns, but rarely as permanent residents, or in number equal to those dispersed through the Eastern counties. Directly between London and the great centres of industry in the Midlands – if we except Banbury and one or two minor places – the Irish element is as thinly scattered as in the East and the West. In the collegiate city of Oxford – the chief centre of English intellectual fosterage and culture, in which the educational light which has never since ceased to illuminate its halls was first kindled from the fanes of the Sacred Island by the hands of monks and "wisdom seekers", who were then the glory of the sanctuaries and the schools – the poverty-stricken wanderers who represent their race and kindred today scarcely find home or hospitality. The race that preserved light and literature in Europe during the midnight of the dark ages, and dispensed them with a liberality and charity as broad and all-embracing as the faith they bore to the strongholds of the Pagan, has been degraded by centuries of misrule from the condition of propagandists and teachers, to the lowest grade of toilers – and accordingly we find them in their numbers and their might only where the willing heart and strong hand can win sustenance in the ranks of labour. From Leicester to Longton – from Bristol to Berwick – there is not a town of any importance which has not its vigorous and flourishing Irish polulation; and here – like the chosen people in their Egyptian bondage – they increase and multiply exceedingly.

Proceeding northward, we first met at Leicester with evidences of that Irish life which afterwards becomes such a marked and powerful element in the population of the midland and northern towns. Here, as chiefly elsewhere in England, our countrymen bear the brunt of toil, and clear away the ruder obstructions in advance of the great army of labour. With few exceptions they are literally the hewers of wood and drawers of water. The English workingman in the towns is generally skilled in some craft, or attached to some calling. The Irishman comes unskilled to England, and hence his destiny has doomed him to the most dreary drudgery. But here, even amid the most adverse and depressing influences, we met with evidences of the force of Irish genius and the power of Irish patriotism. The educated intelligence is limited, because of the position of the people; but the exceptional cases are striking and creditable. The steady and sober of the working classes, in an Irish population of nearly 2,000, is comparatively very large; and among them, in conjunction with a limited number who have arisen from the ranks of labour, the patriotic spirit is marked by the foundation of a Home Rule Association, and the large support, in proportion to numbers, which they give to Irish national literature. The wage-rate is good, and but for the one vice of drunkenness – almost the only vice which degrades and disgraces our people all through England – the social condition of the Irish in Leicester would rapidly improve. That they are eminently free from the taint of ordinary crime is attested by the fact – for which I have the authority of one of the Dominican Fathers, an Englishman, who is chaplain of the jail – that on the criminal calendar for the whole of Leicestershire there is not a single Irish name, and within the borough jurisdiction but three or four, for offences which are the merest trifles – cases of petty larceny or offences arising out of drunken brawls. The Irish population scattered through the whole shire must be something near 4,000. In such a population so small a percentage of crime furnishes the highest evidence of the character and moral worth of the people. Here, as elsewhere, however, a discount must be made for the fallen and lost; but it is trifling in comparison with what is to be found in other towns.

The Home Rule Association, which numbers over one hundred members, is under earnest, energetic, and intelligent guidance, and promises in the future to become a force of much influence in the municipal and parliamentary affairs of the borough. What is wanted here to aid the leaders of the movement in stimulating and extending the organisation, is periodic visits and addresses from trusted and accredited political leaders, who would speak and act in the name of the parent association. This remark applies with equal force to the other towns throughout England. The meetings recently held in the large towns have had excellent results; but something should be done to extend similar benefits to the smaller towns, where in comparison to population the Irish element is equally influential. In Leicester much has been done which is highly creditable to the zeal and patriotism of our fellow-countrymen; and, under the earnest and patriotic guidance which has effected so much, I have every confidence that much more will be accomplished in the future.

Letter VI

13th August, 1872

From Leicester to Birmingham, and we are in one of the most active centres of English political thought – a town as noted for the freedom and spirit of its people, as for the variety of its productions in art and manufactures. Here the Irish population is large, amounting to over 30,000 souls; and here the political influence which the Irish people exercise is most marked and beneficial. There is no interest, local or national, in which that influence is not felt – none in which it has not practically the power – under proper organisation and guidance – to direct the issues and control the designs of party. But here, as elsewhere among the Irish people, there is a lack of that coherent union and persistent energy so essential to the accomplishment of all that lies within their power. Trained in an excellent political school, and prompt on occasion to give evidence that its lessons have not been lost on them, our people in Birmingham have given such repeated proofs of their patriotism and fidelity, that to recite them would be only to repeat what is well and widely known; but they are too prone to relax effort when the occasion which called it forth is past, and so are unprepared to grapple with political contingencies as they arise, or exercise that amount of influence which their numbers, position, intelligence, and patriotism would ensure to them under a well-devised and permanent system of organisation. In few towns in England have the Irish people, as occasion required, come to the front and acted with more decision and effect than in Birmingham, and in scarcely any has there been less previously organised preparation. This shows at once the strength and the weakness – the force and the fault of the people. If so much has been done without preparation, what could be effected if a people so numerous, influential, and intelligent were marshalled in their full force, and prompt, at the instance of their trained and deputed leaders, to act when called upon in the name of creed, country or principle?

Birmingham was one of the first towns in England in which a Home Rule Association was formed – *the* first, I believe, so publicly pledged itself to the principle and purpose of the movement. Since then it has scarcely kept pace with the other large towns. At present the Home Rule Association is being reorganised, and under its new management will, I have no doubt, realise the expectations of its early promise. Patriotism, ability, and public spirit are not lacking. The thing required is to combine these, and direct the whole force furnished by their combination in such a manner as to be practical and effective. To organise a complete system of registration and unite the elements of force thus obtained, to be ready for any emergency, appears to be the first essential preliminary to make the Irish power of the town felt and respected. It would be superfluous to suggest the many ways in which this would prove a source of power and an advantage. Under the guidance of a central body like the Executive of the Home Rule Association, besides furnishing the means of control in municipal and parliamentary affairs, it would bring into more close communion the thought and feeling of the Irish people, and supply one of the best means of counteracting the vitiating influences of English social life. Probably literary and political clubs in all the large towns – the programmes of which would include periodic reunions – would best effect this object. But I find I am directing instead of describing, forgetting, in my zeal to promote the good of our people, that my commision is but to see and to report on their state and condition.

In Birmingham there is to be found a larger percentage of the Irish people who are trained to skilled and artistic workmanship than in most of the other English towns; and here, as in all other cases where Irish taste and genius are cultivated, their peculiar adaptability for the higher kinds of manual art is evident. But the great body of the people earn their bread by the severest toil. Chiefly the young have been trained to skilled labour; and the numbers of those who have worked their way into middle class positions, though considerable, bear no proportion to the great toiling many. In all these classes the best elements of the Irish mind and character are to be found. The zeal – the charity – the sacrifice for others – the purity – the piety, which appear so conspicuously to distinguish the Irish race, is nowhere more marked than here. Indeed, this is true of all the Black Country, which – at least so far as relates to the Irish people – is not so black as it is painted by the Scribes and Pharisees of the Cockney press. But here in Birmingham there is a great loss – a loss that I am assured by an Irish priest who has laboured long and zealously for the welfare of his people, amounting to one in six of the Irish population. Two thousand of the young are on the road to ruin. Three thousand of the adult population in the gloom of indifference. This is the dread total. Their poverty at first drove them to live among the worst of the bad. The force of evil example dragged them to the earth. Some struggle on, good and virtuous to the last – often pinched by poverty and assailed by the most trying temptations. Others, weaker in spirit, yield to the influence of the corruption by which they are surrounded, and sink into its direful depths. The vice of drunkenness ruins hundreds. The force of example does the rest. The youth of careless or intemperate parents – (both male and female) – grow up themselves indifferent, or, it may be, imitate the example of their elders, only to surpass them in their degradation. The youth are taught indifference to parent control by their English associates, and this often in cases where the parents are examples of all that is good. Hundreds on hundreds of the Irish youth here and throughout England are thus ruined. Schooled in vice, they graduate to crime, became absorbed in the ranks of the evil, and are lost. There is no shutting one's eyes to the fact. It is so here – it is so everywhere. There is just this, however, to be said about it which is highly creditable to the Irish of Birmingham. There are few – very few – Irish women who have sunk to the lowest depths of degradation. Though fallen away from what they were, they are not as those to whose example they owe their degradation – though habitually indifferent, they are rarely impure.

But when all deductions are made – and deductions there must be made everywhere in England – the condition of the Irish in Birmingham is one of power and promise. Politically – even in this most Liberal of towns – their power is sufficient to mar the Liberal programme and rule the destiny of an election; and it is a question if at next election that power will not be used in opposition to the nominees of the Education League. Socially, the Irish here are more on an equality and in harmony with the English people than in most other places. Their patriotism is respected. Effort to obtain for Ireland her just rights not alone meets no active opposition, but, in nearly every instance, is cordially aided by Englishmen. Much of this is due to the just and liberal spirit of the people – much more to the earnest labours of a few Irishmen in combatting prejudice and promoting truthful and fair public opinion on Irish affairs – much more still to the work and example of the Rev. Arthur O'Neill – a Baptist Minister here of great local influence – whose power with the people has been one of the chief aids in destroying prejudice and creating good feeling among the English masses; and who never fails to take advantage of the occasion, whatever it may be, to proclaim the injustice of English rule in Ireland, and vindicate the right of the people to make their own laws and shape their own destiny. What has been done here can be done – nay, is being done – elsewhere; and here and throughout England the Irish people are as yet but preparing for the struggle which they are determined to pursue till triumph crowns their labours, and the land of their hope and their affections is a crowned queen among the nations.

The "Black Country" is the distinguishing name given to a district of the English Midlands, noted for its coal and iron mines, and for various and extensive manufactures in the latter commodity – chiefly in articles requiring great strength and not demanding high artistic taste or superior and delicate manual skill. In some districts the manufactures in iron are beautiful and elaborate in design, and the workmanship accurately and highly finished, but generally the description given applies to the chief manufactures for which this district is remarkable. Roughly estimated, the Black Country includes a district of about 200 square miles, extending from Birmingham to Wolverhampton in the one direction, and from Stourbridge to Walsall in the other. All this space is covered with mining buildings – furnaces for smelting the iron ore – and manufactories in which the metal is afterwards prepared and wrought into the curious and multifarious shapes in which it is sent out to the markets of the world. Here can be seen iron work in nearly all its manufactured forms. With the exception of cutlery, there is scarcely any form in which iron and steel may not be seen in this district. From the most delicate needle to the anchor, from the curiously wrought and highly polished "steel toy" to the light-house, the marine boiler, and the iron and steel plates of which vessels are constructed, or by which – in the case of naval vessels – their sides are defended – from the newest and most perfect weapons of death to the most precise and elaborately finished engines of progress and prosperity – ironwork can be seen here in its fullest manufactured perfection, as well as in the various processes by which it is converted from the ore and the oxide into its last stage of finished perfection. Mars and Minerva alike engage the brain of the designer and direct the hand of the workman. On the borders of the district, and in Birmingham and Wolverhampton, the more finished and delicate kinds of workmanship are executed, the coarser and stronger in the centre, which is the "Black Country" proper. In the one case the most cunning machinery has to be employed as well as the highest manual skill. In the other, the roaring and flaming furnace and the ponderous, though precise, steam hammer executes the work. Were the rites of Paganism not abolished, and a temple to be erected to Vulcan, the most fitting site on earth for the gloomy edifice would be in the centre of the Black Country.

This district consists of a series of towns and villages, all linked together by chains of works and furnaces, which make the whole space look like one continuous town. In these towns and villages there is a very large Irish population. Their modes of life and position in any one of them apply generally to all – but for our purpose it will be necessary to note their numbers, position, and power in the chief centres, with the view of forming a just estimate of their present influence and their future prospects.

The position and condition of the Irish population in Birmingham I have pointed out – but this description would not in any sense apply to the Irish in the other towns of the "Black Country". In the former there are various trades and callings in which the Irish people – and particularly the young – are trained to skilled and artistic labour. In the latter, the coal pit, the iron mine, the pit-head labour, and the furnace, furnish the chief sources of employ for the people, both English and Irish. The Irish people, in proportion to their numbers, supply a fair quota to the ranks of the more skilled employees in the manufactories; but the great bulk of Irish labour is either confined to the occupations mentioned or employed by railway companies, builders, &c., in the lowest and most laborious positions, and at a wage rate considerably below what can be obtained by those employed at the mines or in the works connected with the iron manufactures. In Smethwick – which is properly a suburb of Birmingham – in West Bromwich, and Epon Lane, and in the adjoining villages and "works", there is a considerable Irish population – their presence being marked in the two places first mentioned by the churches which they have erected and the missions of which they are the chief support; but not till we come to Wednesbury do we encounter an Irish population having position and power sufficient to make its presence felt and its political rights and privileges respected. Here, in a community in which the associations are both coarse and debasing, a large Irish population assert their rights, preserve their national individuality, and in every particular hold their own. In the town of Wednesbury there are above 3,000 of an Irish population. If the computation be extended to the boundaries of the district comprehended in the parliamentary constituency, the numbers may be set down at over double that figure. It is to be regretted that there is no regular census of the Irish or even of the Catholics in England, so that computations as to their numbers must be based on approximation. Judged by this standard, and on a basis that I have found nearly always accurate in every town I have visited in England – that one Irish voter represents seven of an Irish population – I conclude from the number of Irish voters on the parliamentary register of the Wednesbury polling districts, that the Irish population numbers at least 6,000 souls. This district includes the largest population in any constituency in England; yet here the Irish people feel themselves strong enough to exact from a candidate at next election a formal promise to support Home Rule, as the only condition in which their support will be given. In prospect of this, and under the auspices of the local branch of the Home Rule Association, an Irish census with a view to complete registration is about to be instituted, and the whole Irish population is to be organised and kept in a state of thorough preparation – a proceeding which might be imitated with great advantage by the Irish people living in towns in England. The Home Rule Association here numbers over 100 members, and is under an earnest and practically efficient administration. Indeed, it may be safely said that the political power of the Irish population of this district, all things considered, is – whether as to preparation now or promise in the future – as satisfactory as it could well be expected.

Letter VII

20th August 1872

The labouring population in Wednesbury earn very high wages (indeed, the highest in the whole district) but I regret to say that, in too many instances, the results are in no way commensurate to the boon. Too often the wages earned by the severest toil are squandered in the most prodigal folly. The man who labours in the pit, or broils before the furnace from Monday till Saturday – from Saturday till Monday spends the greater part of the wages of the week. It is so with the entire labouring population – English as well as Irish. The prevailing vice here, and, indeed, throughout the whole of the Black Country, is drunkenneses. For this the people endeavour to excuse themselves by the plea that the nature of their occupation is such that drink is indispensable – and that to drink water only would be highly dangerous. This must be admitted; but I have it on the very best authority – authority founded on long experience, personal and otherwise – that the best drink for those who attend the furnaces or work in the foundries is water and oatmeal. Those who confine themselves to it have more energy and more endurance than their fellows whose beverage is beer, and who have to take it in such quantities to make up for the waste and dryness induced by the excessive heat of the places where they work, that their normal condition is that of semi-intoxication. The result in the end is a habit that is most degrading and detrimental to health and morals. To this state too many of the Irish people descend – and to this, more than to any other cause, is to be attributed the faults and vices by which they are degraded and debased. Here, as elsewhere in England, the sober, industrious, religious Irishman, who preserves his native virtues and avoids the vices by which he is surrounded, is an example of all that is good to everyone with whom he comes in contact, and an honour to his race and country. But, unfortunately, the complement of this native virtue is a dreadful amount of acquired vice which has been nurtured in, and is fed by, drunkenness, and, what is still worse, the vice is nearly as common with the women as the men. The result is very deplorable. All the finer perceptions and feelings are destroyed by it. So are family ties and parental authority. So, too – though one sees little squalor or misery here – are the comforts and happiness of home. But withal, this must be said of the Irish in the "Black Country", that though this vice prevails amongst them to a greater extent than in any other place in England, with the exception of a few of the Lancashire and Yorkshire towns, there is less criminal vice, and notably less immorality, among our people here than I have found elsewhere. The exceptions, if any, are Birmingham and Wolverhampton. But when this is said, it must by no means be inferred that the ruin and loss is not great. Unfortunately, the reverse is the case. Were I not judging by comparison with places much worse, I would say the loss is great. The wonder is that in such a state of society it should be so little. There could be no standard of comparison instituted between the relgious and social condition of the Irish at home and here. This must be always understood. In the best instances a large percentage of the people is on the way to ruin. Nearly all that is good in our people here is Irish. Three-fourths of what is bad is acquired – and acquired from the habits, manners, and morals of the lowest and worst among the English people. I have said before, and I cannot too often repeat it, that it is the fate which drives the people here which is their ruin. To labour to reverse this fate is almost as much a religious as a patriotic duty. Whoever doubts it had better come to England, examine one town – even the best – and then judge for himself. Ponder it well, ye men of Ireland. Protestant of the North, Catholic of the South, on you the duty and the responsibility is equal. The loss is not confined to the Catholic population – nor have I exclusively confined my inquiries to them. the subject is one involving the loss of the Irish people – the disgrace is one that reflects on the fair fame of a traditionally virtuous nation. But no – I am wrong – we are not a nation: provincialism has at the same time destroyed our love of liberty and degraded our manly virtues. If we were a free nation, our poor people would not be scattered and crushed, as they are here, nor would I be following in their track, chronicling their virtues with pride – saddening – maddening – when I see them in the throng and battle of life driven by the force of imperious circumstances out into the dreary and dismal darkness and over the precipice of ruin. It is so; and provincialism has also destroyed the high and chivalrous sense of manly honour in the breasts of the Irish people at home. Otherwise, the manhood of the land would arise and stand as a wall of brass between the agents of the system which produces this ruin and those who have not been yet made its victims, but who may be – nay, inevitably will be – if the relations between Ireland and England be not altered, and the Irish land made the home of the Irish people.

The description which has been given of Wednesbury applies generally to the other towns of the "Black Country", and the position, occupation, habits, and modes of life of the Irish people resident in them are pretty much the same. All the people of the district, English and Irish, are occupied in the coal and iron mines, or in the works directly or remotely connected with these industries, but in nearly every instance the rougher and severer kinds of work fall to the lot of the Irish people. At one time, and not so long since, both here and in Lancashire the English "pit men" refused to permit Irishmen to work in the mines, but now, in this district at least, difference of nationality rarely occasions a dispute, and prejudice never operates so as to shut out Irishmen from sharing in the mining labour of the district. In the North it is the same, and there, indeed, as we shall see hereafter, the chief among the promoters and organisers of labour movements are Irishmen. This, however, is not altogether an unmixed good, for the destruction of the barriers of prejudice promotes a social intercourse which is a curse rather than a blessing to the Irish people.

A series of towns of greater or lesser magnitude, occupying the centre of the system of the Black Country, are almost in every particular counterparts of Wednesbury, Bilston, Swan Village, Tipton, Priestfield, and Oldbury, are, in fact, but loosely-linked parts of a whole. In all these there is a considerable Irish population, though only in the first and last is there the unfailing evidence of an Irish population in England – the mission, the church, and the schools. There is a smaller mission at Willenhall, a town noted for lock manufacture, being between Bilston and Walsall. In this district the Irish population cannot be much short of 5,000 to 6,000. Bilston alone has over 2,000 and Oldbury some 1,300, and the Willenhall district can be little short of this latter figure. The condition of the Irish people through the district, making due allowance for everything, is satisfactory. Their manners are not all that might be desired – their conversation is sometimes the jargon of the mines – there is evidence too frequent of indulgences in strong potations – but, apart from this, the moral condition of the people throughout the whole district is better than in the large towns in other parts of England. A promising feature in the social economy of the district – and one full of hope for the future – is the number and efficiency of the schools which have been erected within the last few years, and in this particular the Irish are abreast if not ahead of the English population of the district. In Wednesbury – thanks to the munificence of an English Catholic clergyman – two noble schools have been erected, capable, I should think, of accommodating 800 pupils; and in Bilston is a large and commodious school, under the management of a zealous Irish priest and the conduct of efficient and successful teachers, male and female. There are Catholic schools also in one or two of the smaller towns. As time progresses, and the seed sown in these schools bears the fruit which they now promise, a great deal will be done to promote a moral and social revolution in the district; but much indeed there is to be done – and much, I am afraid, will remain undone – which the schools cannot touch – or which, if they do touch, the mark of their influence will be afterwards marred by the manners and morals of the pit-head, the mine, and the manufactory.

In Wednesbury and Bilston are mutual benefit societies, under distinctive Irish and Catholic names, patronised and encouraged by the clergy, and productive of much benefit to the poor people in times of temporary distress, or where sickness or accident renders members unable to pursue their ordinary labours. These guilds of the poor have male and female branches, so that the benefit of their operation extends to the whole labouring community. The tendency of such institutions is, of course, to keep the Irish people distinct in social matters, as they are in religion and nationality. The benefits arising from this isolation can only be appreciated by those acquainted with the district and its population. Isolation so far as possible, is the safety and salvation of the Irish people resident here, as well as in the large towns of England. So guarded and circumscribed, the Irish colonies, with all their faults, are the oases in the moral desert by which they are surrounded – occasionally, it may be, blotched with blight and barrenness, for the hardiest plants of virtue are not proof against the pestilential atmosphere – but still, though the tenderest flowers may be nipped, and the sweetest fruit tainted by poison, the Irish centres of population are the brightest of the green spots in the Sahara of English life.

On the boundaries of the Black Country, at Walsall, Wolverhampton, and Kidderminster, there is a slight, though but a very slight, change in the position and occupation of the Irish people, as compared with the centre of the district. In Dudley, lying further within the outline, the condition of the people is pretty much the same. Here, and on to Stourbridge and Brierley Hill, there is a considerable sprinkling of an Irish population; but in Dudley only are the numbers sufficiently large to exercise any considerable political or social influence. In Dudley there is a fixed Irish population of some 1,300 people, possessing a political and municipal power represented by some 200 votes – which, in a town of such limited size, is relatively large. This power, too, they do not fail to exercise as occasion demands; but the organisation and preparation essential to prompt, united action is lacking here as elsewhere. They have the men and the means among themselves, and need but union and purpose to accomplish as much as in many towns of larger population and wider fame. The Irish population here earn good wages, and, in proportion to their numbers, there are more skilled artisans in this than in the other towns of the district. There is also a fair number of men who have raised themselves out of the ranks of labour, and are pushing onwards to comfort and competence. Relatively the moral condition of the people is good. The church and schools are well attended, and everything fair and promising for the future.

Letter VIII

27th August, 1872

The Irish population of Kidderminster is about the same as that of Dudley, but the condition of the people is scarcely so good. They are nearly all of the labouring population, and in the great majority of cases not trained to any skilled craft. The history of the growth of the Irish population here is worth noting, as furnishing evidence of the destruction of skilled Irish industry and the promotion of English prosperity in its ruin. Before 1830 there was little, if any, Irish population here. Tenterdon Steeple, it is naively said, is the cause of the Goodwin Sands. Conversely it may be said that the Catholic population and Catholic Church of Kidderminster are the consequences of the ruin of the Irish woollen trade, so rapidly effected after the Union. This industry, as intended by the English monopolists, and the statesmen who legislated in their interest, gradually languished from the Union to 1826, and more rapidly till 1839, when woollen manufacture, as a native Irish industry, almost totally disappeared. In 1829 and 1830 numbers of wool-combers from Cork – driven from home by the destruction of the trade which was their source of maintenance – came to Kidderminster and found employment in the carpet manufactories for which the town is famous. Thither the Irish priest followed the Irish people – poor, outcast waifs of the wreck of a nation's industry; it was his mission, if he could not prevent their temporal loss, to watch over their eternal interests. The first priest was the Rev. Charles James O'Connor, nephew of O'Connell, who afterwards contributed largely to the fund for the building of the small chapel which then sufficed for the requirments of the congregation, and visited and attended Mass there after its erection. This clergyman has left it on record in his own handwriting – now in the possession of the kindly, courteous, and learned Dr. McCave, the rector in charge of the museum – that he "made the first oblation which had been offered in that town for three hundred years on Trinity Sunday, 1831", in the Methodist Chapel, on the Bewdly-road. "Misery", says Shakespeare, "makes us acquainted with strange bedfellows."[7] The necessities of the Cork woolcombers and their pastor certainly forced them into strange ground on which to scatter abroad the seeds of the Faith in Kidderminster.[8] There is no record to say whether the Methodist Chapel was at the time congregationless. If not, and that the Methodists opened their door to the wandering sheep and good shepherd of the Catholic flock, the deed deserves the most sincere and unqualified commendation. But the event occurred just after O'Connell had struck the chains from the limbs of Dissent, and the gratitude of the people most probably expressed itself in this remarkable example of Christian hospitality. Whatever the cause, the fact is indisputable, and from this small beginning has sprung the Catholic mission with its comfortable congregation – chiefly, almost wholly, Irish – its neat church and commodious schools. Probably there is not in England another mission whose history is so remarkable, or one so suggestive of thoughts and memories so inseparably connected with the wreck of our nation and the name of the man whose great heart broke in the endeavour to reverse the policy of ruin by which Irish industry was destroyed and Irish artisans driven abroad as outcasts.

There are in Kidderminster good, earnest, patriotic Irishmen, but their political influence is not what it might be. Their power, it is true, is limited, but unity and energy could here, out of small means, accomplish much. There are men here capable of the task. All that is wanted is to resolve and act.

Walsall has an Irish population variously estimated at from 4,500 to 6,500. A mean between would probably represent the correct figure. The district surrounding the town is chiefly occupied with mines; but in the town are many manufactories, chiefly in saddlery, harness, and the metal and plated mounts used in these trades. The Irish population is nearly all of the labouring class. A few are just outside the ranks of labour; and a larger number within the circle of the artisan class. But the labouring class earn good wages, and with thrift and sobriety might be comfortable, and, in their own way, independent. There are two Catholic churches in the town with good school accommodation, and everything needed for the spiritual and educational requirements of the people. The Irishmen of Walsall are spirited and patriotic, and exercise considerable influence in the political and municipal affairs of the borough. Marshalled under the banner of Home Rule, and holding their power in reserve for Ireland, they have the power to exact terms for Ireland from aspirants to parliamentary honours when the time arrives to put forth their strength and make their demand. The moral and social condition, and the estimated loss of the Irish population here, are nearly the same as in the other towns of the Black Country – that is, excepting the one vice of drunkenness, the moral condition of the people, considering surrounding circumstances, is higher than generally through England.

Wolverhampton, the northern limit of the "Black Country" – is the last and, after Birmingham, the greatest town to be noted in the great mining district of the Midlands. Its manufactures are the same as the heavier kinds of work done in Birmingham, and its merchants and tradesmen are among the largest and most enterprising in the neighbourhood. The Irish population is large, probably from 10,000 to 12,000, chiefly of the labouring class, but all earning good wages and comparatively well-to-do. Their religious zeal is marked by the churches which they have erected, and the ready support they give to the missions and the schools. There are three churches in the town, with suitable schools attached to each, and these in every instance have been mainly built, and are supported by, the Irish people. Exceptions, of course, there will be in all such cases, but this is the rule. Hitherto, the political influence exercised by the Irish people in Wolverhampton has not been so great as from their numbers one would be led to expect; but the cause has been the same as in all the other towns in England: want of a principle of unity, and an organisation based on that principle and "educated" up to the standard essential for united action at the call of patriotic duty. This want, however, has been supplied, and henceforth the town of Wolverhampton may be regarded as one of the efficient centres of Irish political power in England. The Home Rule Association of the town, which is large and growing larger, is well organised, under intelligent, active, and earnest administration, and supported on financial and general principles eminently calculated to promote its success and efficiency. An electoral census, and registration, where hitherto neglected, is the need of the hour, but this, I am certain, will be promptly attended to, and the power of the Irishman in Wolverhampton strengthened by every means which can make it efficient for the service of Ireland. This I know to be the intention of the founders of the Home Rule Association, and to this I am confident every aim of their patriotic efforts will be directed.

Generally the statement made of the moral and social state of the Irish people in Birmingham will apply to Wolverhampton. Of these two towns, and of the Black Country generally, it may be safely said that in no place under the same circumstances have the people remained truer to Faith and Fatherland than here. In the centre of the Black Country the associations are the very worst, and yet here the moral condition of the Irish people stands superior to what is found in the larger towns. The exceptions – if exceptions are to be made – are in Birmingham and Wolverhampton, but even these towns are exceptionally free from the worst vices when contrasted with towns of equal population in other parts of England. There is no apparent reason for this, but such is the result which I arrive at from much and careful observation and inquiry. That there is ruin and much loss here cannot be denied, but it is comparatively much less than I have seen elsewhere. Destruction is the destiny of the banished; and it is poor comfort and, no cause for exultation to be only able to say that in some instances the destruction is less deadly, and that no race on earth would pass through the same trial with so little loss. This is all that can be said, but how much lies behind all that must remain unsaid when it is only thus we can point to the indestructible individuality and virtues of our race!

Between the "Black Country" and the manufacturing districts of Lancashire and Yorkshire – a geographical space including part of Shropshire, the greater part of Staffordshire, and the whole of Derby, Nottingham, and Cheshire – the Irish population is not aggregated to any considerable extent, though there is interspersed through the district an Irish element numbering thousands. In the town of Stafford, and in the locality known as the Potteries, in the north of the county, are numerous Irish residents, but so scattered as not to constitute a power relatively. Perhaps the whole of this district, south of Chester and Chesterfield, contains an Irish population, numbering from 8,000 to 10,000 souls. The exceptions to this general statement are to be met with in Burton and Derby – the former having a world-wide reputation as the headquarters of the brewing interest – the latter as being a town of considerable historic interest, and in our time noted as the centre of a railway system which is among the first and most prosperous in England. The Irish people have been drawn to these places as centres of employment, and are consequently to be found here in greater numbers than in any other places in the district.

Burton might be passed over but for one or two matters which I think ought to be known. It is, as I have said and the world knows, the centre of the brewing interest – the town in which the monopolists of the beer vat draw the largest profits known on earth from a trade which, of all others, is the greatest tax on the time and funds of the working population. The world will be startled to learn that the wages paid here to those who are mere labourers are the lowest known in England. The average wages paid agricultural labourers, north and south included, estimating increase for particular seasons, and taking into account custom and privileges, is much higher than what is paid by the Burton brewers to their workmen. There is an uproar throughout all England in the name of the agricultural labourers. Not a word has been heard of the inadequacy of the wages of the employees of the Burton beer monopolists. But here are the facts, and the public can judge of the position of the men and the munificence of the masters. Unskilled labour is paid in Burton at the rate of from 14s to 16s a week, and in some instances as low as twelve shillings. This, when deductions are made for rent, is a lower rate than the average sum paid for agricultural labour. Added to this there is the usual allowance of beer, which in the day – if I remember rightly – amounts to a quart or more. The consequence is that poverty, scant food, and beery habits in time do their work, and the result is seen in the manners and morals of the people. There is not in England, in proportion to population, a town in which the average condition of the inhabitants is socially lower than in Burton – and the Irish population have sunk nearly to the level of their surroundings.

There is a historic incident connected with this town which I think should not be passed over by a chronicler of the Irish race. Indeed, it is chiefly because of this incident that I pause in my record to notice the town. There are associations extending backwards for centuries connecting Burton's history with Ireland, which happily are of a higher and holier type than those of today – associations that call to memory the time when Ireland was the school and sanctuary of Europe, and sent out their teachers, saints and missionaries to instruct, civilise, and save mankind. The world knows something of our schools in the dark ages of Alfred's Irish education – the foundation of Oxford, and the schools he established throughout England chiefly through the aid of the saints and "wisdom sellers" of Erin. Our English friends question the fact or deny the extent of the influence exercised. But here is one incident worth a thousand arguments in proof of the reputation for sanctity of the Irish people in the early ages of the Church in Ireland – of the influence they exercised abroad, and the fruit of the labours they bequeathed to posterity.

In the town of Burton the light of faith and piety, which had been quenched in the blood of the people under the tyranny of Danish rule, was relumed by the hands of an Irish saint – the holy and zealous Saint Modwen – who not alone tended the sacred flame in Burton, but carried it to the ends of the island, kindling anew or restoring the light as she passed, in fanes of her own foundation, or those which had been deserted or desecrated. Even the Danish "reign of terror" could not check the holy mission and zeal of the Irish people. Out they poured to meet the barbarous hordes who overran Europe, and with no weapons but the learning of man and the grace of wisdom of God, only met them to chasten and subdue, to instruct and civilise. This saintly Modwen is a type of the Irish saints of the age and the wonderful influence they exercised. The event which occurred towards the close of the ninth century is thus chronicled in the quaint language of Holingshed:

> In this season one Modwen, a virgin in Ireland, was greatly renowned in the world, unto whom King Ethelwolfe sent his son Alfred to be cured of a disease that was thought incurable; but by her means he recovered health, and, therefore, when her monastrie was destroyed in Ireland, Modwen came over into England, unto whom King Ethelwolfe gave leave to build two abbies, and also delivered unto her his sister Edith to be a professed nun. Modwen hereupon built two monastries – one at Poulesworth, joining to the bounds of Arderne, where she placed the foresaid Edith with Oseth and Atha; the other, whether it was a monastrie or cell, she founded in Strenshall or Trentshall, where she herself remained solitarie a certain time in praier and other vertuous excercises, and (as it is reported) she went thrice to Rome, and finallie died, being 130 years of age. Her bodie was first burried in an island compassed round by the river of Trent, called Andressey, taking the name of a church or chapelle of St. Andrew, which she had built in the same island, and dwelled therein for the space of seven years. Manie monastries she builded both in England and Scotland, as at Striveling, Edenbrough, and in Ireland at Celistline and elsewhere.

A quaint and strange record to find in Burton in the end of the nineteenth century, just 1,000 years after the date of the miracles and works of the Irish saint. Since then revolutions have swept the land; the very faith she planted has been proscribed, and its votaries slain or banished as felons; but the work and the memory of the Irish virgin lives in legend and record:

> Only the actions of the just
> Smell sweet, and blossom in the dust.

Modwen's memory is not forgotten, and her action is likely to blossom into a repetition of her zeal in our day, though the fruit must be poor compared to that realised by her labour. The Protestant church is still named after her; the site of her chapel is still called St. Modwen's Orchard; and last, but not least, in an obscure corner of the modern town of Burton is a school chapel dedicated to her name, presided over by a learned and zealous young Irish Levite, where the sons and daughters of Ireland, poor and humble, assemble weekly for worship and sacrifice. Independent Ireland sent out her sainted children to conquer, civilise, and sway by truth, piety, and virtue. From provincial Ireland her children are driven as outcasts, to be gathered together for worship almost on the very sites of the missionary triumphs of their ancestors. What a contrast! What a lesson! But even in the scattered and trampled ones is the seed of virtue and zeal. A new church in honour of St. Monica is contemplated; the ground has been secured, and the pastor of the scattered flock hopes – through the prayers of the patroness, and the generosity of her children in England, Ireland, and Scotland – that he will be enabled to raise an edifice worthy in some degree of her name, in which the Irish population of Burton may one day assemble and worship.

Letter IX

4th September, 1872

Passing northward to the mining and manufacturing districts of Lancashire and Yorkshire, the chief centres of Irish power and influence are Derby, Nottingham, and Chesterfield. The Irish element interspersed with the town and village population of the other parts of Derby, Nottingham, and Lincolnshire is large but subdivided, and scattered in the hamlets and farmsteads lying between Derby and Hull, and still further north, through East Yorkshire, to the confines of Durham. One can only approximate their numbers, which is unquestionably large, but their political power and social influence are so small as to produce little or no influence on the community. The Irish agricultural labourer in England is, indeed, the Pariah of his race – a being whose lot is toil unsweetened by that kindly sympathy and social freedom which nature and custom have endeared to him, and without which he is lonely as the Bedouin of the desert. The towns mentioned, however, have a considerable Irish element in their population, and these, as I have said, are the centres where the semi-nomads of the agricultural districts meet and commune with their own race and kindred. In Derby, with a population of about 50,000, the Irish people muster some 3,000 strong – and here, considering their numbers, relatively their political and social influence is considerable and increasing. Politically they experience little hostility, and for years the town has been remarkable for tolerance in religious matters, and for the kindly feeling and harmony prevailing among all creeds and classes. The Catholic population, which is mainly Irish, has its legitimate influence in the affairs of the town generally, and, in proportion to its numbers and the position of its members, contrasts, in this respect, most favourably with the Irish people in nearly all the other towns I have visited. The church and school accommodation is ample, and on the school board and in municipal matters the Catholic element is represented and respected. It is not surprising to find that the moral and religious condition of the Irish people of Derby is exceptionally good, and that the clergymen in charge of the mission look forward to even a much better state of things in the future.

Nottingham has an Irish population something larger than that of Derby, but – except in the patriotic spirit of a large proportion of the people – in other respects not so satisfactory. Indeed, it may be said that the destructive influences at work in Nottingham are as injurious to the Irish people morally and materially as in any town in England. The Nottingham "lambs" have attained to a questionable notoriety in connexion with election affairs in the borough; but these "lambs" after all, are but the natural offshoots of the community. Roebuck was the proper, because the characteristic, representative of such a people, and till the town returns him again there will be no poetic compensation in its politics.[9] In such a community, and forced by imperious circumstances to associate with the lowest of the population, the condition of the Irish people in too many instances is deplorable. In one district of the town – almost wholly Irish – much has been done by the zeal and practical energy of an earnest and self-sacrificing Irish priest – the Rev. Mr. Harnett – to banish the multiform demons that assail the faith and virtue of his flock. But, though here and elsewhere in the town, the peculiar virtues of the Irish people distingish them from their neighbours, the stamp of vice is too plainly on the community. Drink and evil example are sapping the virtue of the people, and dragging down hundreds to the level of their surroundings. But here, as elsewhere, are found the patriotic, the good, and the true – men whose fidelity to fatherland remains the same through all time and under all circumstances. The branch Home Rule Association is but one evidence of the spirit and patriotic feeling of the Irishmen of Nottingham. Within the association are to be found zealous workers, and trained and long-tried political judgment and sagacity; and still outside of it, too much of the true and sterling manhood, whose co-operation is essential to its influence and power. The requirement of the hour is unity and organisation.

With these, the Irish people of Nottingham can do much to aid the patriotic labours of their kindred at home. Without the preparation, of which these are the elements, the real strength and influence which they possess and can exercise will be but imperfectly applied, and hence lose half its effect.

There is an Irish population in Chesterfield numbering nearly 3,000, and including the surrounding mining district, fully 5,000. The growth of the population is but recent. As a consequence, scarcely any of this large number are to be found outside the ranks of labour; but the wages are good, the average being about 25s a week, and the general condition of the people in other respects satisfactory. There is sufficient church accommodation both in the town and neighbourhood, and the schools are very commodious and in a high state of efficiency. The Jesuit Fathers, who serve the mission at Chesterfield, speak in very favourable terms of the conduct, morals, and habits of the Irish people, as contrasted with their English fellow-labourers in the mines and works. Their one vice is drink. Their honour and honesty are most remarkable. Petty larceny and the class of crimes which come within the jurisdiction of the local magistrates are almost unknown amongst the Irish population of the neighbourhood. There is much, indeed, in the present condition and future prospects of the Irish people of this locality that is hopeful and promising, contrasting most pleasantly with what is to be seen and anticipated of their kindred in other places.

From Chesterfield to Hull, with the exception of Doncaster, there is little of an Irish element to be met with. In Doncaster and neighbourhood there is, perhaps, an Irish population of 1,000; and in Hull, from 5,000 to 6,000. Of this number, with the exception of a few persons employed in the Customs and Excise, all are in the lowest ranks of labour. Indeed, to say that they are low in other respects, too, would be but conveying an inadequate idea of their condition. Here, as elsewhere, are the good, the pious, and the patriotic; but in no other town in England is there a larger proportion of the Irish population fallen and lost. Hull is the only town I have known where whole families have separated themselves in idea and sentiment from their kindred, and, renegades to Faith and Fatherland, have ranged themselves on the side of England and infidelity. The general moral state of the town is low, and the condition of the Irish population corresponds with its surroundings. It would be but painful to particularise. It is enough to say that what is true of the worst part of London applies here, only that the loss is greater in proportion to population. The Irish here have neither political power nor influence, socially. They number less than one-twentieth of the population, and these in the very lowest grade. They furnish, indeed, the worst example of the evils of the exodus, and bring home with most striking force to the mind and heart of the moralist, the nationalist, the Christian, the criminal iniquity of the system that roots out from their home and disperses a virtuous people, and dooms them thus to fester and rot in the vice and corruption of the English towns.

In the towns of West Yorkshire, as in all other places where labour wins bread and perseverance competence, we meet with an Irish population possessing power, position, and intelligence, and exercising in every relation of life a marked influence on the communities among whom they reside. There is but little to vary the lot of the Irish residents in the Yorkshire towns; and the description which suits the one may be taken generally to apply to all. In all, or nearly all of them, the Irish population is so large as to exercise a political influence sufficient to rule the destinies of parties. In Leeds the Irish population is estimated at from 22,000 to 25,000. Including the surrounding districts, the Irish population certainly amounts to the latter figure. Dewsbury has 4,000, and the surrounding districts 3,000, Irish residents; Huddersfield, nearly 3,000; Wakefield, an equal number; Barnsley, 2,000; Halifax, from 5,000 to 6,000; Bradford, from 20,000 to 25,000, in a population of 146,000. In nearly all of these towns the power of political parties is so nearly balanced that, with proper organisation and preparation, the issue of an electoral contest would depend on the Irish vote. We shall hereafter see that the power of the Irish population in the Lancashire towns is still greater. These districts are the chief strongholds of the "Liberal party"; and to these they look with confidence to swell the majority which sustains them in power. Hitherto, in the conflict of parties, the Liberals always could rely on the Irish vote. Henceforth the Irish vote will be held for the service of Ireland, irrespective of the needs of English political parties. To exact conditions for Ireland, or – failing in that – to make government by party so unstable as to be practically inoperative for legislative purposes, should in every instance be the aim of the Irish residents in the English towns. This I have taken it upon myself to advise, and the advice, I have reason to believe, will be acted on wherever the Irish force is sufficiently powerful to decide the battle of parties. Our business is to restore party equilibrium, and prevent either of the rivals from weighing the scale, so that the possession of power will depend on whether we choose to kick the beam and destroy the equipoise of the party. This is a proceeding which, so far, I should think has never entered into the calculations of the rival factions in Westminster. That its adoption is our wisest policy, I think few will doubt. That the Irish in numbers of the English constituencies possess the power to accomplish it is certain. For proof that they mean to do it I cite one instance, the precedent furnished by which is sure to rule in twenty. I quote from an Irish gentleman in Bradford, whose patriotism and eloquence are only exceeded by the keen introspection of his intellect and the sagacity with which he gauges the measure of success in the future by a wise application of the forces we possess in the present. Speaking of the town in which he resides, and having previously stated that the Irish are as one to seven of the population, he says:

> Since the establishment of household suffrage the number of Irish voters (parliamentary) is roughly estimated at 3,000. As the total number of electors in the borough is just over 21,000, the proportion of one-seventh shows itself here also. The strength of political parties in the borough being very nearly balanced, it follows that at the present time, and for so far into the future as this relative division of parties continues, the decision of every contested parliamentary election lies absolutely with the Irish vote. This was proved conclusively at the last election. At that time, however, the Irish in Bradford were entirely without organisation, and the power they

possessed became, in consequence, a source of no small danger. Both parties, aware that success depended on the Irish vote, used the most unscrupulous means to secure it, and succeeded only too well with a large number of the less sagacious and intelligent of our people. By means of sham Irish committees, which were only blinds for treating, &c., *ad libitum*, they managed to degrade and corrupt a considerable number. The election was thereby vitiated and the member (Mr. Reply) unseated. If there had been an organisation capable of guiding the Irish vote, this would have been prevented. The Home Rule Association now promises to supply that great want, and hence its establishment and success have given great annoyance to the leaders of both parties – Whig and Tory alike. They see in the Irish Home Rule Association a rising power which will preserve the Irish vote in Bradford from becoming (what they wish it to be) a mere tool for the advancement of their party purposes.

Hitherto the Irish vote was a constant quantity in the equation of English parties. The Whigs – or, as Sam Slick called them, "the weakest and smallest party, but that which always cheats at cards", and "aint above looking into the hands of their adversaries" – regarded the Irish vote as their special patrimony. But it is not an inheritance of theirs after all. The Irish vote in England is held only for Ireland – and for that purpose, and that only, should it, or will it be exercised. I have no particular affection for the Tories, but I certainly should not regret to witness their restoration to power. They could give us nothing worse than Coercion Acts, Arms Acts, and Press Gagging Acts, nor could they treat with more supercilious contempt the expressed wishes of the Irish people than has our present Liberal administration presided over by "the people's William". Hartington and Keogh are its types and representative in Ireland.[10] The *battue* in the Phoenix Park is an evidence of the liberal impartiality of its administration – the Galway Judgement of its sense of equity. The fitting retribution for its misdeeds will come with the fullest poetic justice from the Irish in England. Their defeat by the expatriated Irish will teach them that even in England, Ireland is a power, and that the people who a few years since were "gone with a vengeance", live to requite the sympathy then shown for their sufferings by bringing home the "Irish difficulty" to their doors, and giving them the most striking proof that the cause of Irish nationality is as irrepressible as centuries of coercion and proscription have proved it to be indestructible.

Letter X

10th September, 1872

There is a great uniformity in the condition of the Irish people living in the towns of West Yorkshire. The employment, habits, manners, and morals of the English people in the towns vary little, and the Irish people here as elsewhere are much influenced by local associations. The chief employment is obtained in the woollen and cotton factories; but the great bulk of the Irish people not being trained to factory work, they must be content to take the lowest place in the labour market, and accept the roughest and rudest work. The women and the young in time find their way into the factories. The men are to be found wherever the hardest work is to be done and wages rule highest. Their social influence is small compared with their numbers, but this is explained by the fact that very few of the Irish people have struggled out of the ranks of labour. Their moral condition corresponds generally with that obtaining among their kindred in the other towns of England – that is, it is good – exceptionally good – considered in relation to the moral state of the English people, but woefully, mournfully low when compared with any conceivable Irish standard.

There are influences at work, impelled and directed by the active, earnest, and zealous energy of priests and people, which in the end must operate generally for the social and moral benefit of the masses, but years must elapse before the seed now being sown produces the desired fruit. Wherever the Irish people have settled in towns – that is in the lowest and most neglected quarters – there arise the church and the school, and thence, as from the twilight in the mists of morning, issue the rays of truth and intelligence, giving full promise of the full glory of the coming morn. A brief summary of the religious and educational means possessed by the Irish people in the towns of West Yorkshire will furnish the best evidence of what has already been done, and what may be hoped in the future of a people who in little better than a quarter of a century, and under the most adverse circumstances, have raised such memorials to their piety and zeal.

Beginning with Leeds, we find four central missions – St. Patrick's, St. Mary's, St. Anne's and St. Joseph's – each having efficient schools, and all being, in the main, supported by Irish people. Besides these, there are three other missions served from one or other of the preceding. One of these, appropriately bearing the name of St. Bridget has its centre and sanctuary in a building rescued from the disciples of a notorious fanatic named Anne Carr, who, some thirty or forty years since, secured a "following" from the offscourings of the Church and the sectarians – a class who, because they believe nothing, are prepared to believe anything – by the most absurd rhapsodies and phrensied assumptions. The revelation of folly had its day; and now, through the zeal and labour of Father O'Donnell, the building which witnessed the pitiable aberrations of phrensied fanaticism is converted into a temple of faith and worship for the Irish people. Leeds is well supplied with churches, and will shortly have ample school accommodation, and no town in England stands more in need of the spiritual and social benefits they confer. Thousands of the people – fully a fifth of the Irish population – are here sunk to the very lowest social level.

Sheffield contains a large Irish population, and one which, if properly organised and directed, might exercise great power and influence; but this essential preliminary to the direction of all political force has been here much neglected. The mind and manhood is here – the unity that gives power is wanting. This defect, I have reason to believe, will be remedied, and then the Irish power of Sheffield may be reckoned on as an important auxiliary in the muster of the forces which in England is certain to be marshalled in the National cause. In other respects the condition of the Irish in Sheffield is highly satisfactory. Socially they are nearly all confined to the ranks of labour, but the moral state of the Irish here will contrast favourably with nearly any town in England. Of course there are sad and disheartening exceptions. Drink has its due share of victims, and the general canker of vice with which the community is tainted is slowly consuming the virtue of too many of our people. But all considered, the condition of the people may be pronounced good. Much of this happy effect is due to the untiring zeal and judicious labours of the Vincentian Fathers, who train up the youth and supervise the social life of the people in a manner highly creditable and eminently efficacious. Nothing, indeed, could be more admirable than their schools, or more worthy of praise and imitation, than the careful paternal interest which they take in all that concerns the members of their flock. The youth they watch and guard – the family they advise and direct. "This we can do", said the Superior to me, replying to question as to the secret of his success, "because we have a sufficient number of priests, and each attends to his special duties; but it would be impossible to do as we do in an ordinary mission, where the priest is distracted by a multiplicity of duties without time to attend to the half of them." This is, indeed, the sad and simple truth. What a boon and a blessing would it be to the Irish in other large towns in England if their faith and morals were fostered and guarded as in the case of those who have the good fortune to live under the spiritual care of the good Fathers of St. Vincent at Sheffield.

There is a uniformity in the moral and social condition of the Irish in the smaller towns of West Yorkshire. In Dewsbury, Huddersfield, and Wakefield their condition may be regarded as satisfactory. In Barnsley – the chief, almost the only seat of linen manufacture in Yorkshire – the condition and position of the Irish population strongly contrasts with their prevailing state in other towns. Here are to be found many Irish people outside the ranks of mere unskilled labour. In the weaving and bleaching establishments the best workmen are skilled hands from Ireland. Few are rich – but none are poor, and all are in comfortable circumstances. The head of the largest bleaching firm in the town is an Irishman – so is the best pattern weaver. The superiority of Irish intelligence is shown by the fact that an Irishman presides over the Literary Association – an institution open to all creeds and classes, and in which the most cordial harmony prevails. The teacher of the Catholic school – acknowledged to be the best in

Yorkshire – is an Irishman. A greater man in his own way than any of them is Casey – known through the north of England as the "King of Colliers".[11] He is indeed their advocate and administrator – in everything their "guide, philosopher, and friend". He rules the most powerful union in England, and has secured the faith of his following by the energy and ability with which he watches over their interests. His name is sufficient evidence of his nationality. His merit is to be found in the fact that he has risen from the ranks of those he rules, and this notwithstanding the prejudice prevailing against him as a Catholic and an Irishman. His success, though humble, is worthy of record as furnishing a striking illustration of the native force of Irish mind, even in the circumstances most unfavourable to its development, and supplying a trenchant rejoinder to the class of English critics who condescendingly credit Irish intellect with every faculty but those necessary for organisation and ruling power.

In Bradford and Halifax – though there is much to be seen only to be deplored – the state of the Irish population is satisfactory. In the former town, as I last week noticed, the Irish possess great political power. The Home Rule Association there, though established only since last January, numbers nearly 700 on its rolls, and the accession to its force goes on regularly increasing. Here is evidence of great political power, but up to the present the results have not been proportionate to the means. There are Scotchmen and Germans in the Corporation and on the Board of Guardians; but no Irishman, or even an English Catholic. There is no Catholic magistrate in the town. Two Catholics – one an Irishman – represent 25,000 Catholics on the School Board. This is scarcely satisfactory; but there are healthful and hopeful evidences that the policy of passiveness which has hitherto prevailed will no longer be tolerated, and that the full organised force of the Irish populace will be henceforth directed, in both local and imperial affairs, with the view of advancing Irish interests in the town, and controlling the influence of parties in the interests of Ireland. There is not in England a town where there are Irishmen better qualified to organise and direct the people politically, and none, I am satisfied, from which, in proportion to population, the national cause will receive more efficient aid.

The position of the Irish people in Bradford is, in very few instances, above the rank of the lowest labour. The men are chiefly employed as builders' labourers, excavators, &c.; the women in the mills, in the worsted manufacture. Of their conduct and condition Mr. J. O'Neill (the gentleman from whom I quoted in my last letter) thus writes: "The Irish mill-girls in Bradford are a very worthy and respectable class. As a rule, they are very attentive to their religious duties, and very well conducted. There are exceptions – but they are *exceptions*, and only show off by contrast the good conduct of the majority." He notes it, and notes it with the sympathetic regret of patriotic friendship, that there exists "a very great apathy amongst Irish parents with regard to the education of their children"; that they are content that they should pursue the same dreary drudgery as they themselves have been compelled to from want of early opportunity; and says that in consequence "a vast amount of nascent talent and ability in Irish boys is allowed to perish for the want of even ordinary education and opportunity"; but this neglect, I fear, is not confined to Bradford, but generally prevails in all the English towns. "The general morality of the people," he adds, "even in the midst of all the debasing temptations of an English town, still marks them off as a distinct and superior people." The one prevailing vice is drunkenness. "If that horrible and debasing evil could be exorcised from our midst, then not even the most prejudiced English observer could fail to be struck by the superior morality and goodness of our people – their charity, their patience, their cheerfulness, and their immovable Faith." This testimony is as true as it is high, and applies to the Irish in most of the English towns in a greater or lesser degree. But with all this goodness and virtue there is the waste, the loss, and the ruin everywhere. Bradford may be exceptionally favoured; but when the balance of evil is struck, and the favourable contrasted with the foul, there will be found small cause for congratulation or comfort. Bradford, indeed, contrasts more favourably with other English towns, but how would it stand if compared with the population of the towns in Ireland?

In Halifax there are more marked evidences of evil than in Bradford, but the general condition of the Irish population is satisfactory. The vice is drink – the faults of the people its consequence. Their moral condition, apart from this, may be considered good. Ordinary town labour for the men-factory work for women and children, supply the means of employment. The wages here, as in the other towns of Yorkshire, are good, and the means at the disposal of all who will work are ample. The Irish, who number from a sixth to an eighth of the population, have given evidence of their local power by returning their member on the School Board, and under the banner of Home Rule are organising their strength for the broader labour of the parliamentary contest. There is here a considerable floating population, so that to estimate political power by a numerical test would lead to error. But the political strength of the Irish people in Halifax is considerable, and under judicious control might produce highly beneficial results. A re-organisation of the Home Rule Association so as to secure unity within and harmony without, will supply the means to effect this. The spirit and patriotic devotion of the people is unquestionable. The need of the hour is organisation and a constant propagandism in the principles upon which the Home Rule Association bases the rights and claims of Ireland. The Irishmen of Halifax posess the means to efficiently aid the national cause. Communion in sentiment, and perseverance in preparation, are alone required to make these means effective. There is this to be said, too, in favour of organised and united action – and the observation applies with equal force to the Irish population in every town in England – that the combination which gives them power politically, secures to Irishmen an influence socially to which as aids and supports of English political factions they never could hope to attain. Power of wealth are the measure of an Englishman's respect, and the Irish in England will be respected just in proportion to the evidence they furnish of their unity and invincibility in the hour of political trial.

Crossing the conventional boundary between Yorkshire and Lancashire, and making Manchester the objective point, the important towns of Rochdale and Oldham intervene, the former having an Irish population of over 5,000 in 60,000, the latter of over 10,000 in 99,000. In these towns, though the Irish element is relatively so large, the political influence they exercise is less than in the Yorkshire towns, and much less than can be brought to bear on the other towns of Lancashire. This is chiefly due to a lack of political leadership in communities almost exclusively made up of labourers and factory hands. The remedy for this defect could be best supplied by periodic visits from recognised representatives of the national party commissioned to organise the people and indicate the political action essential to efficiency and success. In many places in England some such course is necessary if all the constituents of our power are to be combined and made effective. There is more than sufficient intelligence in every community of Irishmen in England to pursue the right path when once it is indicated. In many are to be found, combined with the most sterling truth and integrity, an intelligence and political sagacity equal to anything of the kind to be met within the kingdom – much superior to what one meets among Englishmen in the same social grade. But in too many instances their acquirements and gifts are unfruitful of results. The spirit that promotes organisation is a stranger to the community. The mind that could breathe and infuse it into the people is needed. The inspiration that animates – the example that excites emulation – are required to quicken into life and rouse to energy the slumbering spirit of the people. Organisation and agitation are the means to political success, and these never spring spontaneously in the public mind. They are the fruit of the thought of the few and the action of the multitude. In most of the towns in England the full measure of the success which should result from our strength can only be secured by stimulating the people and guiding them in action. In such towns as Rochdale and Oldham, where there is lack of leadership locally, the stimulus of guidance from without is absolutely essential to secure the results which force of numbers alone would otherwise render certain.

Letter XI

17th September 1872

The Irish people of Rochdale and Oldham are now well supplied with schools and churches, though the educational benefits of the one, and the moral and religious effects which should flow from the other, are not so manifest here as in other towns I have visited. The truth is that as soon as the Irish come over to England and settle down in the towns, their whole existence is a struggle against vice, their daily life is in community with crime which tests the most tried virtue. When it is considered that years elapsed before the spiritual care needed to check the growth of moral evil could be supplied to them to anything like the extent needed, and that the opportunity of education is quite a modern blessing whose fruits are as yet scarcely perceptible, there is nothing to be wondered at, though much to be deplored, in the condition of our poor people in these and most of the other towns of England. The cause of the loss explains and palliates the conduct of the lost. The evil has been more in the past than it is in the present, and the change from the lower to the higher state of educational eminence and spiritual good, though slow, is gradual and certain. Forty years ago the Catholic population of Rochdale was scarcely 200. In the towns of the district there were, if not then, a very few years later, from 6,000 to 7,000 Catholics, chiefly, if not entirely, composed of Irish labourers. There was but one priest for this large and scattered community. As to school accommodation, there was none. The priest visited certain centres in succession, and managed as best he could to gather together the scattered ones of his flock. No wonder that many were lost, and nearly all, down almost to our own day, remained uneducated. The town of Rochdale now has an Irish population of from 5,000 to 6,000 and the district formerly served by one priest embraces an Irish population of 20,000. All were poor, but the fervour and faith of the Irish heart overcame every obstacle.

The town of Rochdale alone has now two missions, St. Patrick's and St. John's, supplying accommodation for 2,000 people. Attached to each are schools capable of amply accommodating 1,000 children, and the remainder of the district is equally well supplied. In Oldham, too, there is fair, if not full, church and school accommodation. Indeed, the prevailing feeling, as one contemplates the change which has been wrought in some twenty or twenty-five years, is admiration of what has been done out of the poverty of the poor. We may regret that more has not been done – that we are not in a position to wrestle with vice and strangle it in its stronghold – but no one can blame or censure the poor, because out of their poverty they have not wrought financial miracles; nor their clergy, because, in consequence of that poverty, they have not been able to realise the full fruition of their zeal and sacrifice. The moral and religious condition of the people here is comparatively good. The evils are drink, and ignorance due to the unfortunate circumstances of the past. Education – in its highest and proper sense – is the cure for both these evils. The regeneration of the people – the hope and promise of the future – is to be found in the schools, and with these, I am happy to say, Rochdale and Oldham are very fairly supplied. Financial impediments here, as in all poor communities, may for a time impede the path of educational progress, but the education and consequent elevation of the people cannot fail to result from the advances already made.

One enters Manchester but to find himself at home in the midst of his fellow countrymen. Here is the first place out of London in which I find an Irish population so numerous as to be a power in the community. Here in the great capital of the cotton trade is an Irish population superior to that of Cork or Belfast. Every fourth man you meet in Manchester is an Irishman. In the city alone, in a population of about 400,000, there are of Irish birth and blood over 100,000. Including the suburbs and surrounding towns and works within a radius of a few miles, there is an estimated additional Irish population of 25,000 to 80,000. Southwards to Chester – taking in Stockport, Warrington, and Macclesfield – a further estimate of from 12,000 to 15,000 may be included. A corresponding average proportion of Irish to English prevails in nearly all the manufacturing towns of Lancashire. In Liverpool the proportion is over one to three. In Wigan nearly one half the people are Irish (*i.e.* 18,000 in 40,000). Throughout the whole of the shire the Irish number at the least one in six of the population. The consequence is that in political matters, if the Irish people do not hold the key of the position in every urban constituency, the fault must be their own. They have the numbers, the votes, and the influence sufficient to dictate terms to political rivals. In most of those towns the political forces are nearly balanced. In few, if any, is either side so strong as to be able to carry its man in opposition of the Irish people. In all the Irish power is influential – in nearly all that influence is paramount. An instance was last week furnished in Preston, though it furnishes one of the most unfavourable examples in the whole of Lancashire. The "Liberals" fancied that by prescriptive right they could count on the Irish vote. It is probable that the Tories, too, made the Irish power an element of antagonism in their calculations, and believed that their success would be much less marked than it has been. A Catholic Committee sat in the interest of "Liberalism". They even endeavoured to "draw", by meeting in public and pledging themselves to support Major German, the Liberal candidate. Whether the Irish people were at all represented in the committee I have not heard; but the names of those reported as appearing on the platform were, with one exception, unmistakably English. What I confidently anticipated – indeed, what I had recommended in Preston and elsewhere – came to pass. The Irish voters refused to pledge themselves, and the Conservative candidate triumphed at the poll.[12] *The Times* next day informed us it was "understood that many of the Irish who were stated to be in favour of Major German either withheld their votes entirely or gave them to the Conservative candidate – a circumstance which has since furnished matter for bewildered comment to the provincial Liberal press of England, who foresee the collapse of their party, and know that the Irish have the power to make or to break it. In Preston, which has always been under the thumb of the Stanleys, the Conservatives have long had the upper hand. But the new franchise and the protection of the Ballot entirely reversed the position of parties, as would have been unmistakably proved had not the outrages perpetrated on public right and individual liberty in Ireland alienated the Irish people, both here and at home. Gladstone and his government can hardly fail to recognise the first touch of the finger of the Irish Nemesis in the Preston election. When the time comes for exercising the full force of its retributive energy, he will find that he has to contend with a power sufficient to shatter the hopes and render futile the schemes of himself and his party.

As I was not on the ground, I cannot, of course form an accurate judgment – but I fancy from the reports that in Preston the example set to our "Liberal" rulers should have been more striking and decisive. Here and everywhere we should speak with no uncertain voice. Our action should be as ordered and compact as serried flies in front of an enemy. If we can – well and good – dictate terms and exact pledges from candidates to support Home Rule or any other measure favourable to Ireland, let our influence and votes by all means be the equivalent for such support. But, failing in this, our next duty is, when occasion offers, to teach such a lesson to those who have trampled on public right and outraged public feeling in Ireland as will serve as a salutary admonition for the future. Ejection from their strongholds in England – and that by the Irish vote – would conjure up before the "Liberal" mental vision a perpetual notice of "cease to do evil, learn to do well", as plain and permanent as the inscription on Richmond Prison, to warn them that the demon of depotism is their most dangerous enemy, and that the Irish in England are quite powerful enough to pay back insult and requite coercion. This we should not alone be prompt to do, but be so organised as to render action efficacious, and always ready to proclaim our determination, and the "why and the wherefore" of our conduct. The action which was partial in Preston, pursued in Lancashire and West Yorkshire, the North, the Midlands, and London, will be certain to dictate a new line of conduct to English statesmen, and teach them that their expectation of holding office without the consent and goodwill of the Irish in England – that is, without granting to

Ireland the full and complete justice of self-autonomy – will prove but a vain and unsubstantial "dream of ambition".

Take Manchester as an instance of what may and should be done if the national question is to be advanced beyond the confines of vague generalities and into the region of fact and action. Political ideas to be valuable must be practical; and the political material being at hand, it would be criminal neglect to let pass a favourable opportunity for using them to advantage. Success depends on idea in action – when action is justified by the possession of means and appliances. This, I maintain, is the case in nearly all the large towns in England – unmistakably so in the great majority. Manchester has an Irish population of 100,000 in 400,000, possessing a political power represented by 12,000 votes. Provided there is organisation and union, what party can presume to represent this great city in opposition to the will of the Irish people? Nay, what is to prevent the Irish population of Manchester from putting forward and returning their own man? Apart from the Irish vote, there are not over 50,000 electors on the rolls. In proportion to the Irish voters there ought to be but 48,000. There is hardly a question that when the election arrives every seat will be contested, and there is equally little doubt the rival parties will be so nearly balanced that the majorities will be but trifling on either side. That is, the total voting power of the constituency will be so subdivided, and the subdivisions so nearly equalised, that none of them can come within from 2,000 to 4,000 of the aggregate Irish vote. What, then, is wanted in the very heart of England – in the city of Free Trade Conventions and Corn Law Leagues – the centre from which Liberalism formerly hailed as the Mecca of its political fanaticism – and where the unorthodox Tories have since entered and taken possession, to wrest from both parties one of its strongholds – nay, the very citadel itself? Nothing but preparation and resolution. The power of numbers is there. The power that organisation gives is wanting. This is in the hands of the people. The last Home Rule demonstration proved what the Irish people of Manchester could and can do. Looking at that magnificent meeting from the platform, the prevailing impression in my mind was, that the people who could do so much could do still more. Subsequent inquiries into their estimated political power convinced me that my instinctive impression was correct. There is in my mind no doubt that, if the relative estimate of population furnished me be within any reasonable limit correct, the Irish people of Manchester have sufficient power, not alone to exact terms for Ireland from English parties, but to call on an Irishman to stand in their name and carry his election triumphantly. Unite and organise – canvass and act – and the thing is done. If I have a doubt on the point, it is that the voting power may be overestimated. But granted this to be correct – except Whigs, Liberals, and Tories, forget their instincts and combine in opposition to the Irish candidate – a contingency by no means probable – the Irish people are sufficiently powerful to secure his return.

What has just been said furnishes ample evidence of the power at the disposal of the Irish in Manchester. That this power has not been made the most of is proved by the lack of Irish representatives in the Corporation and on the various local boards. This is not entirely owing to the absence of an Irish middle class – for though the great body of the people are labourers, artisans, and factory hands, there is a considerable number whose positions would entitle them to aspire to representative honours. The want of Irish representation in local affairs is due, in fact, to the absence of Irish organisation – the want of an *Irish Party* in the town, which could command respect for the Irish people as a body, and be ready on every occasion to champion their cause and advance their interests. The Irish people in any town in England, while divided into sections, and attached to English parties, are practically powerless. It is only when united, and acting as a body, that they secure influence and respect. In Manchester the organisation essential to political success would also promote local influence and social respect.

The Borough of Salford, with a population of over 100,000 has nearly the same relative proportion of Irish as Manchester, with probably less political and local power; but in other respects their position and condition are nearly similar. The political power of the Irish in Salford is at any time sufficient to decide the rival ambitions of parties. Since the Tory reaction in Lancashire, the Liberal camp must admit an enemy if they are hostile or divided. Hence, they are the arbiters of fate in party contests – or, rather, they would be if, banded together and standing aloof from all parties, they declared their determination to hold the power they possess only in the name and for the service of Ireland.

When one considers the wretched condition in which the Irish population came here, and the enormous difficulties they have had to contend against, their condition furnishes matter rather for commendation than reproach, even when the worst is seen and known. This is particularly the case in relation to their constancy in religious matters, and the evidences of their pious zeal which meets the eye wherever one turns in England. The hundreds of churches and schools which have sprung up on the most wretched districts of the large towns within the last twenty years are striking evidences of their superior spiritual and mental nature. No other people on earth out of such great poverty would have accomplished half so much. This is more strikingly apparent in old settlements, such as Liverpool, London, and Manchester; but everywhere there are evidences of zeal – everywhere the magnificent charity of the Irish heart is revealed in its works. In Manchester there is no lack of churches and schools, but still the population increases, and new requirements necessitate new demands, which are always cheerfully complied with. I wish this applied to all – but, alas! there as elsewhere the curse and the canker are at work, and the lost and the fallen are to be counted by thousands, the numbers bearing nearly the same proportion to population as prevails in London and elsewhere. This is the sad supplement to all praise and all merit wherever one turns. The curse of the expatriated is too often desolation and death, and not less often a fate that is darker and sadder still. The vice of the system which drives out the people grows and triumphs in Ireland. In England its victims sink to vice and ruin. Thus it is here – so it is everywhere.

Letter XII

24th September, 1872

Liverpool – the great emporium of British commerce – has, with one exception, a larger proportion of the Irish element in its population than any town in England, and immeasurably a larger proportion of Irishmen who have risen to position and influence. Here one meets with Irish merchants and Irish manufacturers – Irish doctors and Irish lawyers – Irish tradesmen and business men of all classes – Irish priests and Irish teachers – to be counted by the score. Here the Irish people are represented on every local Board and Committee – even to the bench of magistrates. Here there is an Irish power ramifying through every class and grade in the body social and body politic – so strongly rooted and broadly spread that no power and no interest in the town can declare itself independent of it. Here, where the commerce of the whole world finds the most active centre – where, if ships equal to the whole mercantile marine of the greatest commercial nations of the ancients were gathered together in its docks, one-half of them would remain empty – in the town to whose commerce the united trade of Venice and Genoa, in their palmiest days, would bear no comparison, and which now floats an annual tonnage well nigh double that of any other town or city in the world except London, the Irish people possess their fair share of the wealth, power, and distinction that ever follow in the track of commerce. Whatever could be done by the exercise of energy, industry, superior business tact, and intelligence of a higher order than exists amongst the English people with whom they come into competition, has been accomplished. Indeed, everything considered, the Irish people in Liverpool have attained to a degree of prosperity and power eminently creditable to their industry and force of character – eminently discrediting to the fictions of the insolent libellers who deny that the Irish people possess the qualities essential to material success. Of the Irishmen who have attained to wealth and position in Liverpool, there is not one in fifty who has not risen from the ranks of labour – and risen, too, in opposition to prejudices and various hostile circumstances such as no other member of the community has had to encounter and overcome. In nine cases out of ten, even the educated Irishman on coming here had to undergo a noviciate of toil before entering on the comparative ease of superior employment, and then every step upwards was due to his native energy and ability. On reaching the level of comparative prosperity, the Irishman in Liverpool – indeed, throughout all England with very few exceptions – can look back with calm, conscious independence, and proclaim with honest, manly pride that what he possesses is due to the exercise of his own powers, and that no man can say that to him he owes assistance in building up the fabric of his fortunes. There may be exceptions, but they are very few. What I have said applies almost universally. In fact, were it not individious to do so, I could point to a hundred instances in which Irishmen have won independence in this town by the sheer force of their own merits – whereas I know not of one instance in which success has been due to extraneous assistance. We shall see as we proceed that, apart from those who chase fortune on their own account in the various callings and pursuits to which they have devoted themselves, that the offices requiring the greatest amount of energy, care, sagacity, organisation, and direction, are, in the great majority of cases, filled by Irishmen – a clear proof that to these positions they have forced their way by merit, and merit alone. Of course, the great mass of the Irish people here, as elsewhere, are to be found in the ranks of labour. A statement of the Irish population in Liverpool – its relative strength as compared with the English – and a brief analysis of its memebers, classified as to calling, will best show their power and position – what they have done – and what they can do.

The total population of Liverpool may be put down in round numbers at 500,000. The Irish element in this aggregate is variously estimated at from 180,000 to 190,000. Taking the smaller estimate, the Irish inhabitants of Liverpool number over one-third of the entire population. It would be difficult to give an estimate numerically of the political force possessed by this large body of Irishmen. There is no complete organisation to watch over and direct Irish political power – no thorough registration – no scrutiny of the registers to show the extent of that power. But estimated by the standard that I have found everywhere to prevail in England, the Irish population of Liverpool must possess from 20,000 to 24,000 votes. This would give a political force immeasurably superior to that which any candidate could command at an election, even though none of the seats were contested. In case all were contested, the Irish power would be overwhelmingly superior. Politically, then, the Irish people in Liverpool have a dominant power in the politics of the borough. Their political and general intelligence is not alone equal, but superior, to that of their English fellow-townsmen. They have the numbers that constitute strength, and the ability from which springs leadership – everything, in fact, but organisation and community in action to constitute a power superior to any Irish population in England. Such a power organised or held for Ireland – and Ireland alone – could not fail of triumphant success. If a doubt could be entertained about Manchester there can be none at all held in reference to Liverpool. With preparation and united action they can accomplish all they desire. That they mean to do so I have every assurance. That the men who have taken the task in hand will do their utmost I firmly believe. But the sooner intention resolves itself into action, the more assured will be the certainly of success. A combination of the Home Rule Association with the other Irish organisations in the town, a complete registration, and the united direction of the Irish vote, and our countrymen in Liverpool can unquestionably return an Irish member of parliament. I am not myself of the number who believe that Irish representation in the English parliament will effect a change in the policy or purpose of Imperial legislation. Much less do I believe that representation alone, whether in or out of parliament, will ever lead the English people or their rulers to concede Irish legislative independence. But I maintain that the very best policy, even for those most sceptical in reference to legislation in an English parliament, is to wrest from the hands of English parties their most important constituencies, and prove to them and to the world that the Irish people in England have the will and the power to defeat them even with their own weapons and on their own ground. No evil can and much good may result from pursuing this policy. We sacrifice nothing either of principle or position by so doing, but will be almost certain to secure many solid advantages. In this pursuit the Irish people in all the large towns can do much. In Liverpool they can accomplish more than in any other town in England. To be represented in the English parliament by an Irishman is their right. They have the power. Be it their duty to secure it.

The political power of a people is, in a great measure, dependent on their social condition. What that condition is, in respect of the Irish inhabitants of Liverpool, may be judged from the following statistics of the social state and calling of the entire body. I give the figures, merely stating that they were furnished to me by men thoroughly acquainted with the town, and their accuracy afterwards corroborated by a gentleman who, for a quarter of a century at least, has been the advocate and representative of Irish Catholic interests in Liverpool, and who now worthily exercises magisterial jurisdiction in the town where his sterling merit has secured him the grateful regard of his fellow-countrymen, and the respect and esteem of his fellow-citizens of all creeds and classes. Your Lancashire readers will at once perceive that I refer to Mr. James Whitty. To the general reader it may not prove uninteresting to add, that Mr. Whitty claims descent from the early Anglo-Cymric settlers in South Wexford, who, in time, became "more Irish than the Irish", and have ever since been distinguished for their consistent fidelity to "Faith and Fatherland".

The 180,000 Irish in Liverpool are, in our approximate estimate, thus classified: merchants, and holding first-class positions, 300; merchants of the second class – merchant factors, &c., 1,500; shopkeepers, &c., 3,500; clerks, 3,500; stevedores and master-porters and warehousemen, 2,500; skilled artisans, 15,000; commercial assistants, 2,000; men holding professional positions, clergymen, schoolmasters, doctors, and lawyers, 800; market people and street-sellers – a class almost exclusively Irish 2,000; miscellaneous, not living by manual labour, 2,000 to 3,000; living by unskilled manual labour, 146,900. Thus we see that in Liverpool there are from one-fifth to one-sixth of the Irish population who are above the ranks of ordinary toil – a proportion which most strikingly exemplifies the intelligence, industry, and good conduct of those who have risen, when we consider that all, or nearly all, had to force their way from the lowest ranks and against the most adverse odds. Some of those who now occupy positions of trust and importance must, I am informed, be men of great judgment and natural as well as acquired intelligence to fulfil the duties of the offices committed to them. The large class of stevedores and master porters (who are almost to a man Irishmen), require a high order of intelligence as well as trained adaptability to their duties. So important is this class, and so essential to the daily requirements of the mercantile affairs of Liverpool, that a dispute with the merchants, ending in a suspension of work, would, for the time being, upset the whole commercial economy of the town. There are, besides the classes enumerated, numbers of Irishmen in official positions – such as the Customs, Excise, Post Office, &c.; and many of the largest firms have Irishmen in the highest positions – such as managers or their immediate subordinates. Some of these I know personally to be men of superior intelligence and high integrity. Of the entire class of Irishmen acting as commercial assistants, I am informed no men in the community are more freely trusted or can be more firmly relied on.

The Docks furnish the Irish labourers with a market for the only commodity they have to vend – *i.e.* strong arms, broad shoulders, and brave hearts that are cheerful and jocund in the midst of toil. The whole line of docks, extending nearly six miles, swarms with Irish life. The leading men in the sheds – the first in many of the warehouses – the strongest men at the wrench – the most enduring in the stifling ship's hold or the laborious and exhaustive sack-carrying, are Irishmen. There is, in truth, a marvellous amount of Irish power to be seen in the Liverpool

Docks. The faint-hearted and the weakly endure not long; they are crushed out to make room for the resolute and strong – men full of heart and energy, who laugh at labour. But these in their turn become worn out, many by excessive toil, more by hard living combined with hard work. Many drop into easier positions when unable to bear the severest toil. Others pass into the hospitals to linger and die; some attain to higher positions; some begin as small tradesmen, and gradually rise. And so the process of mutation goes on. Men pass away and others supply their place. I think I am not over the mark in stating that two-thirds of the Liverpool dock labourers are Irishmen. To add, that among them are the men most noted for strength and endurance, is to say only what is known to every stevedore and warehouseman from one end to the other of the line of docks.

There is great mortality in the ranks of the dock labourers – partly owing to the nature of the work, partly to insufficiency of food and irregularity of labour, and in a great measure to irregular and intemperate habits contracted in their work and its associations, the whole resulting in waste of energy and waste of life. The average duration of power to stand the hardest work in the various kinds of labour, roughly approximated, is as follows. Corn-heavers and corn-carriers, from ten to twelve years; coal and salt-heavers, nearly the same; working at the winches, technically called "jigger" work, five years; general labour fifteen years. Few men are to be seen in the dock after the age of fifty; but many of these, incapacitated from severer labour, find employment as bag and cotton menders, watchmen, or in other light situations, requiring attention and care, with little labour. But much of the dock work is unhealthy, and all of it very laborious. The result is that men are worn out here more rapidly than in most other kinds of employment. Even furnace work in the mining districts is more healthy and less exhaustive than Liverpool dock work.

The religious and educational requirements of the Irish in Liverpool are very well attended to, and all that zeal and labour can effect for the safety and preservation of the people is done in their behalf. Here the Irish people themselves have, in nearly every instance, furnished the means, and Irish priests and Irish teachers, following in the footsteps of the people, have been mainly instrumental in fostering the intelligence and preserving the Faith of their countrymen. But whether furnished from English or Irish sources, the evidences that the Faith is vital and progressive, and that the means for the education of the people are not wanting, meet the eye at every turn. There are twenty-three Catholic churches, ten convents, and seven monasteries in Liverpool. These have all, or nearly all, been built, and are now supported, by the zealous charity of the Irish people. The rich contribute their pound; the poor, their pence; and so churches and schools have risen in evidence of the constancy in faith and the loving thirst for mental cultivation which has ever distinguished the Irish people. The church accommodation – one church to 8,000 population – can scarcely be deemed sufficient; but the school accommodation is almost, if not entirely, equal to the requirements of the time. A careful examination of the School Board statistics show that the Catholic population of Liverpool have provided school accommodation in elementary schools, industrial schools, and reformatories, for 22,369 children; or for about one in eight of the Catholic population – a proportion which in a community such as this, where a larger proportion of the people remain unmarried than in most other towns – is found to be ample for present requirements. These statistics only supply information in reference to schools within the borough. Outside this boundary there are several large schools, public and private. There is probably school accommodation in and around Liverpool for 25,000 children – certainly for a larger number, if we include Birkenhead and the smaller places on the other side of the Mersey.

This shows a very satisfactory state of things as regards the means for the spiritual and intellectual advancement of the Irish in Liverpool. But when one turns to the effects produced up to the present, the spectacle presented is deplorable indeed. In no town that I have visited – not even excepting Hull – are there more striking evidences of vice and degradation than are here to be seen. By day wrecks of humanity – male and female – degraded and worn out by the dread canker of vice and drunkenness are to be seen in bye-courts and at street corners – grimed and horrent – more like spectres in a distempered dream than beings formed in the image of the Maker. By night vice in a hundred forms is to be seen in the bye-ways and thoroughfares with no constraint on its effrontery and no effort to conceal its hideousness. The drunken laugh that grates painful on the ear – the tongue that addresses the casual passenger in the language of vice and coarseness – is too often in the tone of the poor degraded Irish girl, who, far from home and friends, guidance or protection, sank into the vicious vortex which swamps virtue and destroys the bodies and souls of thousands in such a town as this. Alas, that vice and ruin should track our people wherever one turns – that in the midst of the rejoicings of the heavenly hosts the Angel of Mercy would have to turn away with averted face to weep for the fallen and the lost. If true generally, how much more true of the expatriated Irish that, though

> Some flowers of Eden we yet inherit,
> The trail of the serpent is over them all.[13]

But who can judge of the purpose of it all? Who knows the ways and can gauge the mercy of the Inscrutable and Infinite?

Generally it may be said of the Irish in Liverpool that, taking man for man and class for class, the spirit and patriotism of the people is equal to that existing in any part of the kingdom. A few become "respectable" and flunkefied, and fade into the limbo of the weak-souled and the harmless. But the great mass of the Irish people are sterling, true, and manly in the highest sense – Irish in heart, sentiment, and soul – and as earnest and intelligent as they are patriotic and true. There is no class here like your inane Dublin "fashionable", a hybrid between the professional parasite and the Belgravian sybarite – the class that John Mitchel scorched by his sarcasm and "Shamrock" lashed with a keenness of causticy unequalled since Swift. They know not here your simpering fop or "gentle dastard". There is here the material and the brain of manhood – strong enough, true enough, intelligent enough, for all the requirements of effective political work. Their power is manifest. The secret of converting its hitherto latent force into a most potent auxiliary for winning the independence of their native land is comprised in these words – unity, organisation, and action.

I perceive that in two separate and indeed entirely opposite quarters the letters of your Special Commissioner have this week been producing a gentle flutter of doubt and trepidation. The writers in some of the provisional "liberal" press of England have been noting our work and deprecating any tendency to defection from their standard. They judge of the future by Preston, and feel not at all comfortable as they forecast and discount the future. On the other hand, the *Tablet* is piously and philosophically endeavouring to convince us that we ought to forget differences of nationality and only remember that we are English Catholics. Well, well, the one may fear and the other moralise. I can only furnish both with this assurance – not very consoling, I admit – that, when the time comes to prove it, both will see that the Irish in England are attached to no party but to Ireland, and that, though Catholics to the core, they will never be won from their "Irish ways", and acknowledge themselves Englishmen.

Letter XIII

1st October, 1872

Before I turn from contemplating the condition of the Irish in Liverpool there are one or two points demanding attention as furnishing matter for hope and promise in reference to their future, particularly as regards the youth of the poorest classes down to the little abandoned waifs who, till recently, without parent or protector, found a home in the streets, and food and shelter after the manner of the ravens of the desert. I refer to the means which have been adopted to check the drunkenness and preserve outcast children from the pains and perils of their desolate lot. With these two evils – intemperance and the poverty which is, in nine cases out of ten, – its consequence – one man, the Rev. Mr. Nugent, has taken upon himself the high and holy task of waging a war of conquest and rescuing the people, old and young, from the demons of death and destruction that are ever their attendants and executioners. There could be no higher mission than this. To battle with vice and rescue its victims is a struggle worthy the emulation of angels, the benedictions of heaven, the praises of all men. And this is truly what is being done in Liverpool. Father Nugent may be said literally to bear the banner of Temperance with one hand, while with the other he gathers together the poor little houseless Arabs of the streets, and leads them to the home of peace and comfort, security and salvation, which he has provided for them. With a zeal that never flags, an energy that never tires, and a devotion to his mission which inspires and animates both, he is found labouring wherever virtue is to be promoted or a victim to be rescued from the serpent clasp of vice. Today he is directing or leading a temperance meeting, tomorrow exhorting the Catholic inmates of a reformatory, attending to the duties of his chaplaincy, or, mayhap, discussing with some local board or committee the claims he has on the public funds in aid of his Boys' Home. This month you hear of his being in Canada or the United States, making provision for the future settlement of his children. You have only time to wonder if he has succeeded, and speculate as to what the future of the fatherless and motherless orphans may be, when you hear that he is away in Ireland with his orphan orchestra – *à la* Professor Marks and his little men – giving concerts in the various towns in aid of the funds required to support the Orphans' Home. In Liverpool there is – God knows – room and work enough for many such labourers. *One* can but stimulate the zeal of the few and the charity of the multitude. But this one, by his energy and example, has already effected incalculable good. The thousands of children he has already rescued from the streets have been snatched from vice and crime, and trained to virtue and industry. Who can calculate the benefit of such work to the rescued and to society? He who saves a life in peril is appropriately commended and justly rewarded. He who produces two blades of grass where but one grew before, is declared on high authority to be a public benefactor. What, then, is to be said of the man who saves hundreds – thousands – of his fellow-creatures from the perils of vice, converts them into good and intelligent members of society, and – what is to him a matter of much higher importance – directs them in the way of saving their immortal souls?

These are among the agencies at work in Liverpool for reforming and saving the Irish people from the evil habits and effects of intemperance and the sufferings and perils of poverty. With the young the success is most consolatory. The Young Men's Societies and the various Catholic Confraternities and Guilds are the centres in which are fostered and the sources from which flow the hope and promise of the future. The effort to abolish intemperance is verily a struggle with a demon whose name is legion. To check its career tasks the highest effort. To grapple with and crush it, would be the task of a man competent to work miracles.

In Wigan, with a population of forty thousand, there are, as I before observed, 18,000 Irish forming the highest relative proportion of Irish to English population of any town in England.

Of this large number nearly all are labourers or factory hands. A few have worked their way into the ranks of the lower middle class, and a still larger number are small traders and skilled artisans. In the surrounding district many are employed in the pits and iron works, usually in positions where labour is hardest and wages least. Nearly half the pit-men in the neighbouring coal and iron works are now Irish, though, till recently, the English miner refused to work beside the Irishman, and hatred and hostility marked nearly every relation of the men of the one nationality to those of the other. The effects of this commingling both in the mines and in the iron works and cotton factories on the manners and morals of the Irish people are extremely evil. "Their manners are the grossest, their language abominable", were the words used by my informant to express his sense of the example and its effects. But withal the moral and religious condition of the Irish people resident in Wigan contrast favourably with their kindred in other towns. Judged by the clergyman's test of the number who attend church and conform in every way to the requirements of their duty as Catholics, the proportion of those who might be classed as good stands exceptionally high. Notwithstanding the contaminating influences by which they are surrounded, and the effects of the evil example which was before their eyes from childhood, the Irish youth of both sexes have preserved themselves singularly free from the taint of vice. This may be in a great measure due to the zealous care with which the children are first trained in the schools and afterwards watched and guarded. The school accommodation at present is quite ample to supply the needs even of a larger population. In a population of 18,000 schools sufficient to accommodate 3,100, or over one in six of the whole people, is a proportion larger than I remember meeting elsewhere. There is also church accommodation sufficient for the requirements of the community. There are four churches in the town, and two missions have been established in the immediate district to meet the requirements of from 1,000 to 2,000 persons employed in the surrounding mines and works. The total Irish population of Wigan and district may therefore be estimated at nearly twenty thousand, and this, though the Irish population of the town and immediate neighbourhood was reduced 2,000 by emigration during the "cotton famine" consequent on the war in the United States.

The political power possessed by the Irish in Wigan is not proportioned to their numbers. The same may be said of their social and municipal influence. This is, without question, due to want of organisation and leaders springing from the people themselves. In no town in England is this more apparent. Within a few miles distance, in the town of Bolton, an Irish population of but 15,000 in 120,000 possesses double the influence in every respet. In Wigan there is certainly the raw material of power, and I am aware that Irish spirit and patriotism exist there in abundance. But the mass is inert and inoperative, because not organised and animated by the spirit of a higher intelligence. To point out to the people their power, and direct them in the proper use of it is all that is required. The spirit and patriotic fervour of the Irish heart and mind will do the rest. The low standard of political organisation among the Irish people in Wigan may be gauged from the number of names on the register. In a Catholic population of 18,000 there are not over 1,500 voters registered. There should be 2,500 if the proportion to population prevailed here as in other towns. In Bolton there are 2,000 in 15,000. This is a defect which should be remedied. I know there are many good and patriotic Irishmen who heed not English politics, and therefore refuse to register, or, if registered decline to vote. This feeling should exist no longer. For the first time, the Irish people in England have in their power either to cast their vote in favour of their country, or at least to harrass her enemies and frustrate their designs. It is the duty of all to do so, however we may differ on minor points. The Irish in Wigan ought to possess a dominant power in the politics of the town. Let them unite and prepare, and they are certain to secure it. They are at present regarded as a community of inferiors, beneath, though within the circle of English society. An instance of executive consideration and amiability, or it may be of an incapacity to rule the people otherwise, related to me by one of the priests in the town – himself an Irishman – gives the clue to the position occupied by the Irish in Wigan. The magistrates here make it a point never to interfere between priests and people – regarding the Catholic clergymen as their best aids in suppressing vice and promoting good feeling. Appeal is made to them in all cases of extremity, and the consequence is that there are very few petty cases arising from disputes among the Irish people brought before the Bench. Now this – though good in its way – furnishes a proof of the estimate put on the Irish population of the town by the authorities, who may be regarded as representing the opinion of the community. Were the Irish people an organised power exercising its proper influence in the town, and directed by its own leaders, this condescension on the part of the authorities would be unnecessary, and the Irish people would hold and retain their fitting place in the community, in virtue of their own strength and the self-respect which the possession of independence and power always inspires.

In Bolton – as I have said – the condition of the Irish people is very different. I have alluded to their numbers and political strength. Their social influence here, as everywhere else, is proportionate to their political power. The great mass of the people live by labour; but here are Irishmen of position, intelligence, and influence, who have made themselves felt in local affairs, and are well competent to make themselves felt in the affairs of the nation. What the Bolton people are fortunate enough to possess is wanted to the men of Wigan – *i.e.*, Irishmen of position who are at the same time competent for political and local leadership. Till the establishment of household suffrage the Irishmen of Bolton were scarcely in a position to make their power felt independently. But the power once being within their grasp they seized and used it at the first opportunity. That opportunity was presented by the School Board elections. At these elections the Irish vote, judiciously directed, secured to the people their fair share of representation on the Board – and in the person of one of their members – Mr. Healy – a representative eminently qualified to watch over ever Irish and Catholic interest. From the papers lately I see that at the pending municipal elections the Irish people are putting foward three candidates, and consider their power sufficient to carry them all. This is the result of organisation and intelligent leadership. With the same preparation and equal ability in direction, what has been done in Bolton could be accomplished in twenty other places.

I have no knowledge of the relative strength of the rival political parties in this town, but I fancy that the Gladstone and Lowe connexion is scarcely strong enough to have over 2,000 votes deducted from their total and added to the roll of their rivals.[14] If we have any spirit or manhood left this is certainly what should be done. If the Irish people in England or elsewhere are proof against the supercilious cynicism and insolent impertinence of Lowe, as manifested in his Glasgow harangue, and will again support him or the party to which he belongs, why I can see no reason why the gentle complimentary amenities of Keogh at Galway should call forth such severe animadversions. Certainly I think the men of Bolton will know how to requite the Minister who hawks the stale fish of his chief and endeavours by spicing it with sarcasm to make it grateful to the not over-fastidious nostrils of his Scotch auditors. Lowe is a historian, and knows – or ought to know – that *malapropos* jests have more than once led to bloody wars and decided the fate of dynasties. If he live long enough, I fancy we will be able to furnish him with an opportunity of profiting by the teaching which he appears to have overlooked, by showing him that the small matter of the overthrow of a Ministry may depend on causes analogues to those which have led to the destruction of Empires.

In Bolton the Home Rule Association, which Lowe fancies he can wither with a sneer, numbers over 200 members and represents a political strength equal to ten times that number. The organisation is under efficient and able management and the work of political preparation advanced and progressing. When the time comes for exercising their power little will be wanting, and less still in the spirit and wisdom by which it will be directed.

The social and moral condition of the Irish people here is in conformity with their state generally in Lancashire. Intemperance and improvidence are their prevailing failings – the influence of the factory and the mine their greatest enemies. But, everything considered, the condition of the people is declared to be satisfactory by those who have the best opportunity of judging – *i.e.*, the Catholic clergy, particularly when these are Irish – for, all other things being equal, wherever the Irish priest is found with the Irish people there are their morals highest and faith soundest. The churches and schools are sufficient for present requirements. Indeed, as to the schools, the demands of the future are amply provided for by the recent purchase of a large and commodious building, capable of accommodating 2,000 and equally suitable for the requirements of education, for reading-rooms, and for public purposes. There are already 2,000 Irish children on the School Board rolls, a proportion which, in a population of 15,000, shows that here there is little lacking in the provision made for the education of the people. The same may be said of the provision made for their religious care. There are four churches, or one for every 3,750 of the population; and to this circumstance, "and to the fact that we manage to always keep the people under our eyes", said a zealous Irish priest, in reply to my inquiry, "we may, under God, attribute their exceptional virtue and security". There is little, however, to show that our people here differ in these matters from those resident in other towns, and much to be seen only to be deplored. In every place we have to confront evil, and in the best our only consolation is that we can discount ruin, and place the small gain to the credit of Irish virtue.

The total population of Blackburn is 82,000. Of these 11,000 are Irish, all or nearly all of whom have settled here within the last 25 years. The political force of his body is represented by 1,500 votes, and there are beyond this several Irish names not on the register. This large proportion of votes to population shows that the Irish of Blackburn have attained to a high state of comfort and competence, and that their position in the town should be one of commanding influence. This, however, can hardly be attained without organization, though there is more real unity here, and, as I am informed, greater tendency to act in concert when an emergency arises than is to be met with in other towns. Of course this will always be due to the personal influence and public spirit of a few men of whom the people rely, and whose leadership they are ready to follow unquestioned. But such a condition in a community is always precarious and unstable. What is wanted is that community in organization which does not wholly depend on individuals, and a propagandism of the opinion and sentiment common to all, and of which each should be, according to his power, an active and zealous missionary. Everything is done in our day by calculation and preparation – nothing left to chance or enthusiasm. A lesson from our enemies will direct us the right road. They calculate and prepare all, and, winning or losing, calculate and prepare again. This is what we require. This is what should be done by our good and patriotic friends in Blackburn. Our brethren there have numbers, manhood, intelligence and every requisite element of success. I think, too, I know the men who have the will and the power to organise and direct the whole body of the Irish people in the town. Need I say more than to add that duty demands as the first and most essential condition of effective action the necessity of organization and preparation.

There are in Blackburn four Catholic churches, attended by eight priests, four of whom are Irish. There is sufficient school accommodation, and little wanted for the intellectual and spiritual advancement of the people. The Irish missionary and the Irish teacher are to be found side by side labouring for the salvation, the enlightenment and social advancement of the people, and, as in all other cases when these influences are found in co-operation, with the most marked success. The clergyman who has grown grey in the services of his Maker, and the pious and zealous young missionary who is just entering on his career of labour and love, both bear testimony to the superior virtue, zeal, and devotion of the Irish heart and mind. They have their guide and confraternities for the young – the evening schools for their instruction – the Sunday schools and Sunday influences to draw them from evil and lead them to good. The result is a high state of moral and religious excellence amongst the Irish people as compared with all their surroundings. All that can be done to instruct, direct, and save them is attempted, and if not always successful, the fault lies in the curse of their condition. There are here, as everywhere, the fallen and the lost. The blight, the canker, the curse of expatration is to be seen here and everywhere.

Letter XIV

8th October 1872

Public opinion in England has been for a few weeks past moved and perturbed by the Preston election and its accompanying incidents. On the one side the assumption of cunning and mystery, with just such a judicious display of simulated frankness as was necessary to irritate the defeated party, contributed to invest with undue importance what was, after all, but a commonplace transaction; and on the other, the fears and the ignorance of the facts of the case exhibited by the defeated party and their organs in the press give the affair a serio-comic character to those who know the facts and care not a fig for the issue. The one party is jubilant over nothing – or, at the most, over a victory not due to themselves. The other is philosophically engaged discussing fictions and shadows, while the reality, which apparently they are anxious to ignore, is under their very noses. The former has been first in the hunt, and, thanks to their unexpected allies, have secured the prize. The organs of the latter in the press – like a badly-trained pack – hark and howl on the wrong scent, and in their bewildered stupidity get dispersed, each pursuing the fiction of the writer's vagrant fancy. The one exults in a Tory triumph. The other whines in mystified inanity, and cries out in its humiliating sense of despondency that the ballot-box is at fault and the Ballot Bill a failure. Both are wrong, though the one has some cause for rejoicing. The election was won by other than Tory strength. The influence on the election, attributed to the so-called "card-trick", is the most palpable humbug. By such a scheme the Tories, if they could implicity trust their men, might at any time during the day be able to approximate their own aggregate vote, but this is all – they certainly could not more than guess at that of their opponents; nor could they be confident of success – provided the whole constituency voted – except they were certain of securing over half the votes. Now, in Preston the whole constituency did not vote. The Tories could not have known those who had resolved not to vote and, therefore, could not make any deduction to enable them to arrive with anything like accuracy at the half of those who did vote. The card trick was only a test to mark their own men – probably the scheme of employers anxious to maintain their "legitimate" influence in coercing the employed. The efficiency otherwise attributed to it was an after invention designed to irritate the defeated. The *Times* told the truth when it stated that the election was turned by the Irish electors either declining to vote or voting for the Tory candidate. The fact is that Preston was always a Tory stronghold. The "Liberals" fancied on the recent occasion they could carry it by a *coup-de-main*, with the ballot-box for a breastwork. So they could, too, if they had not outraged and insulted Ireland. The evidences of their having done this are too notorious to need particularising. The result was, the Irish in Preston turned their backs on the camp of the coercionists and slanderers of priests and people, and Major German went into the contest only to be defeated.

If I have given more space to this matter than it appears to deserve, I have not done so without a purpose. In the first place, it has, I understand, been regarded in some parts of Ireland as a precedent which, if followed by the landlords, will secure to them under the Ballot the exercise of the same undue influence as they possessed before the passing of the Act. This is quite a mistake. The Preston election furnishes a precedent for nothing, and only supplies an evidence of how a people may be deceived and imposed upon by any specious sham that seems to lend support to their prejudices or their fears. Cards, it is true, might be imposed on tenants or others. Where is the guarantee that the electors will vote by the card, and where the test by which it can be ascertained whether they may have done so or not? To attempt the trick would be simply to prove its failure. In Preston the boasted accuracy was all guesswork, which in a small constituency, when the rival parties are pretty evenly balanced, could hardly be far out. In a large constituency, whether urban or rural, the guesswork founded on such a test would prove to be the wildest and most inaccurate.

There is, however, a point more important than this – because it concerns the action of the Irish in England and their influence on the English policy of the future – to which I wish to direct public attention. The policy pursued by the Irish in Preston was not that best calculated to assert their power or establish their influence. The organization that makes unity, and the subsequent movement *en masse*, were wanting. What one did, all should have done. I am not now discussing the right or the wrong of the course pursued; I am simply recording an opinion – which I think I share in common with all who think on the subject – that whatever course of action may from time to time be resolved on, the Irish people in England should be prepared to act in a body. There should be no hesitation – no division. Sudden and irresolute preparation to meet an emergency is, no doubt, the cause of want of united action. But this is really the state of things to be deprecated and remedied. Nothing should be left to the accidents of the occasion – nothing to chance. All should be regularly organised, marshalled, and ready for direction. Whether the decision be afterwards prompt action or "masterly inactivity", it matters not. There is the organised Irish power ready at the direction of its self-elected leaders to decide the fate of party, or, if so decided, all to fold their arms and look on with calm indifference while the game of party is being played out. In any case, the conduct of the Irish should prove to the people among whom they live that they are united and determined, and to the minions of party that they hold their power for Ireland, and are not to be diverted from their purpose by any of the specious tricks of expediency adopted by full-blown or nascent politicians ambitious of power, and desirous of securing their support to attain to it. The fate of parties in England is in the hands of the Irish population in the towns if they wisely use the power they possess. To do this, organisation is absolutely and indispensably essential. In some places, much has been done in this way. In others, though it does not appear on the surface, the elements of organisation exist, and could be easily combined into an effective power. In no place is the organisation as general and perfect as it should be. In such places as London, Liverpool, Manchester,

Bolton, Bradford, Leeds, Halifax, Nottingham, and Newcastle, as well as generally through the "Black Country", considerable progress has been made in the work of organisation and preparation. But, while towns like Sheffield, Barnsley, Huddersfield, Dewsbury, Wakefield, Rochdale, Oldham, Wigan, Blackburn, and Preston, remain without any publicly recognised political Association, the process of preparation must be admitted to be imperfect. There is no less patriotism, intelligence, and power in the latter towns than in the former. They lack only the organisation necessary to make the separate elements of power which they possess a concrete political force. The want of this could be observed in Preston. Is not the hint sufficient to induce the action which will prevent a recurrence of such a state of things in the future?

Of all the towns of Lancashire, Preston was that one from which the least political result could be expected if we gauged influence by the test of numbers relatively. But the equipoise of parties rendered a comparatively small number relatively powerful, and in this simple fact is an admonition and a lesson. Power is not always in proportion to numbers, but its effect consists in utilising it all and exercising it with judgment. In Preston, with a total population of 95,000, there are only about 8,000 Irish, or a little over one in twelve of the population. The political power they possess may be represented in round numbers by 1,000 votes. (I am, however, informed there are many who possess the franchise, but are not registered.) But this comparatively small number, or even the half of them, in all ordinary political contests, is sufficient to decide an election. Hence their relative worth, and the importance of combining and using all. Preston is the place where there is just the spirit, the manhood, and the resolution to do this. But the Irishmen of Preston require putting into practice the political philosophy enshrined by Davis in one of his most earnest and spirited ballads:

> The patient dint and powder shock
> Can blast an Empire like a rock.[15]

As you are living and exercising your functions as a journalist beneath an enlightened and "Liberal" Government that wisely limits license in the press by a wholesome Coercion Act, lest I should jeopardise your liberty and your property for want of being perspicuous and definite, I may add that I use the quotation in a metaphorical sense, and am by no means suggesting that preparations are being or should be made to blow the British Empire to fragments. Just now I merely advise our friends by patient preparation to be ready for other purposes. The overthrow of a Ministry is the wildest act we contemplate at present. I have no practical experience of the working of your Coercion Act; but as I know that its application is entirely in the hands of the Executive, I am not clear whether a zealous and irresponsible functionary might not consider himself safe in subjecting you to pains and penalties for constructive conspiracy against the stability of a British Ministry. On this side of the Channel it is the amusement of the populace and the favourite – because interested – game of party. On your side, and under the Coercion code, I know not what interpretation may be put on it by the functionaries of the Castle Bashalic.[16]

In Preston the religious and educational requirements of the people are well provided for. There are seven Catholic churches, attended by seventeen priests, and the school accommodation is, I am informed, ample for all present requirements. The consequence is that, whatever may have been the state of morals and education in the town in the past, the appliances of the present furnish a guarantee of promise for the future. But even in the past, Preston was more favourably circumstanced in this respect than many of the other towns where the Irish people were induced to settle down. In the neighbourhood of Preston there existed previous to the Irish immigration a moderate English Catholic population, so that the Irish people were not entirely destitute of spiritual and mental instruction when they first settled down in the town and districts. The effects of this even now can be seen, and forms one of the items of calculation in the estimate which I venture to make as to the future condition of the people.

There is in Preston a fair Irish middle class, considered in relation to the number of our countrymen permanently settled in the town. The great bulk of our people are employed as labourers or in the cotton factories. In both employment is pretty constant and wages fair. The vices and the losses are the same as are to be met with in the other towns of Lancashire.

An estimate of the Irish population of the principal towns of Lancashire furnishes but a very inadequate idea of the number of Irish residents who have made it their home. The same remark applies with nearly equal accuracy to West Yorkshire. In my journey through the former shire I was accompanied on part of my round by an Irishman long resident in the district, and whose quaint humour is only surpassed by his generous heart and genuine patriotism. He is well acquainted with the Irish in the towns and in the villages, in the mines and in the fields. He knows every kind-hearted Irish *soggarth*, Irish patriot, and considerable Irish population from Lancashire to Liverpool. To my inquiry as to the number of Irish in Lancashire, his suggestive and characteristic reply was:

> Who can tell? They are everywhere. Why, man, there is not a town, nor a village, nor a field, nor a lane in Lancashire where you'll not find them. Wherever there is industry, there they flock. Wherever an honest penny is to be earned, you'll find them. That factory standing away from any town or large village has probably a third of its hands Irish – maybe they walk two or three miles to and from their work. In the coal and iron mines they are gradually working out the Englishmen, who are less hardy and enduring. In the factories, in spite of poverty and prejudice, they are gradually attaining to position. They are in every specious of public and private employ, from the dock and the wharf to the farmstead. If you go into the towns, there they are in thousands. If you follow the river or the stream up into the mountains, be sure those you meet on their banks are one-fourth Irish; and even if you go up among the rocks, them you'll find. Ah, sure, man, we are everywhere, and they can't do without us or keep us down.

And this is literally true. I cannot follow our people into the remote haunts where my good friend assured me I would be certain to meet our kith and kin, and so can only arrive by approximation at the total Irish population of Lancashire. Roughly estimated they make up, I am convinced, one-fourth, or at the very least one-fifth, of the entire population of the shire. I can only show by a general summary how they are scattered, and generally approximate their numbers in some of the smaller towns of Lancashire and northwards to Carlisle.

In the vicinity of Preston, including Blackpool and Lytham, there are 4,000 Irish. In Barwin, 2,500. In Accrington Church and Enfield 3,000. In Burnley, 7,000. In Haslington, 3,000. In Rosindale and Bacup, 6,000. In Ramsbotham and Toddington, 3,000. In Bury, Haywood, and district, 7,000. In Ratcliffe and Pilkington, 3,000. In Clitheroe, 3,000. In Crossley, 4,000. In Lancaster, 2,500. In Ormskirk, 3,000. In Warrington, about 7,000. In Barrow-in-Furness, 1,500. In smaller places and outlying districts in Lancashire, over 4,000. The people in all these places are now well supplied with churches and schools, and have within their reach the elements of prosperity and success. What they had to struggle with before, from the resources of their daily toil, their cumulative charity enabled them to make provision for the erection of the churches and the schools, I can only leave your readers to conjecture.

Many of these places, and others not specially noted, would demand more than a notice *en passant*, did not space and general considerations relating to my commission preclude me from more lengthened reference. One or two remaining places, however, I think merit the distinction of special notice. In St. Helen's, near Liverpool, nearly a third of the population is Irish – the proportions being 15,000 in 47,000. They are for the most part unskilled labourers employed in the chemical and glass work for which the town is noted. It will be easily understood that the Irish in coming here have had to commence in the lowest and most laborious places, and if they rise at all must do so in virtue of their superior power of physical endurance and high mental and moral energy. Without these qualities they could not have risen. That they possessed them is proved by the fact that many have risen to the position of foremen, some to the post of managers, and a few have become manufacturers. The liberal paper of the town is owned and edited by Mr. R.A. Drumgoole, an Irishman. The wealthiest coal owner and chemical manufacturer, Mr. David Gamble, is also an Irishman. The Irish element is well represented among the class of clerks, book-keepers, and cashiers; and on press, besides the proprietor and editor just mentioned, there are Irish reporters and others representative of a higher order of Irish intellect – "all men", says an able and well-informed gentleman well acquainted with the district, "who stand well out from the rank and file, and are much respected and trusted".

The political power of the Irish in St. Helen's is not proportionate to their numbers, the reason being that many are unmarried men living in lodgings. At the last election, they of course supported Mr. Gladstone, who then was the champion of Disestablishment. In the future they will doubtless learn, like their kindred elsewhere in England, that whatever power they possess should be held and used only for Ireland. They need political instruction and local organisation. The rest may be safely left to their national feeling, and the example set them by Manchester and Liverpool. The informant before quoted says that "if all those in the town who have a right to votes claimed them, and if the people were properly instructed to vote only for those who promised unequivocally to support Home Rule, the political power of the Irish in St. Helen's would be quite sufficient to decide an election". Adjoining and included within the municipal boundary is Sutton, which contains the largest glass works in the world. Here the Passionist fathers have a church, monastery, and schools. In St. Helen's are three Catholic churches, and one at Paisley Cross adjoining, with schools attached to each, supplying sufficient accommodation for the youth of the town and district. Attached to two of the churches are good libraries. There are besides two convents and a sufficient number of clergy for all the spiritual requirements of the town. To be told, after this enumeration of spiritual and moral agencies, that the condition of the town was satisfactory, is only what one would be led to expect. Still there are the usual failings and vices, the common loss and ruin. The besetting vice is drunkenness; the cankering spiritual evil, indifference. The example and surrounding here, as elsewhere, produce their pernicious effects.

Widnes and Runcorn, on opposite sides of the Mersey, are two other places to which I think it profitable to turn, though not incorporated towns or possessing any special political significance. The former, in a population of 19,000, has 8,000 Irish; the latter, in 17,000, has 3,000. This large proportion of Irish furnishes sufficient reason for a special reference. The occupation of the people in Widnes is nearly the same as in St. Helen's, with the exception of the glass works. Here the occupation is chiefly confined to chemical or "alkali" works. There is a larger proportion of the Irish people here confined to labour than in St. Helen's; but in other respects the general condition of the Irish population is similar. There are, however, some who have worked themselves to higher positions. Three or four of the hardest-worked and most popular doctors in the town are Irish. So are many foremen, and some of the managers of works. There are two Catholic churches, with schools attached to each, to meet the spiritual and intellectual wants of the people. In all other respects, the statements made in reference to St. Helen's apply equally here. In Runcorn, on the opposite side of the Mersey, there are very few of the Irish inhabitants above the ranks of labour; but both this place and Widnes are quite new settlements. This, no doubt, explains why few Irish people have as yet worked their way upwards. There are a few small shopkeepers and mechanics, but scarcely numerous enough to merit distinguishing from the mass. There is said to be insufficient church and school accommodation in Runcorn for the requirements of the people. There is but one church, and this is said to have a small and poor congregation – a circumstance which rather points to indifference on the part of the people than to any want of accommodation in either church or school. There is in this district, no doubt, the elements of future power and progress, and the large percentage of Irish in the population marks it out as a centre where Irish example and influence may effect much. The raw material of power is here. The leading mind and plastic hand are required to direct and shape it. These, indeed, are necessary adjuncts to success everywhere. Here they are absolutely indispensable. Could Ireland afford the means to organise her children in England, they could be moulded into a political force competent either to exact conditions of the broadest freedom for motherland, or make stable government in England impossible.

On the northern border of Lancashire and lying within Westmoreland is a mining district where a considerable Irish population is permanently located. The mining district lies chiefly in the neighbourhood of the Lakes – the principal centres being Ulverstone and Coneston. These districts, with Whitehaven and Maryport, contain an Irish population of over three thousand. North of this to Carlisle the Irish population is sparse and scattered, but all through Cumberland, in the villages and small towns, a considerable Irish element exists. The wandering Irish labourers in the agricultural districts have become an extinct institution. Landlord law and the "Crowbar Brigade" have made the source from whence they were supplied a desert.[17] The groups that did the hay and harvest work for the English farmer and for a period enlivened their dull homesteads are no more to be met with, or are seen only like late and deserted birds of passage who have been left behind by the flock. Even in agricultural England we can see traces of the ruin inflicted on the Irish people by the "curse and crime" of the alien rule. It was poor enough in the past to know that the Irish peasant had to wander here to seek the means to meet the exorbitant demands of the land harpies who exacted from him an equivalent for his holding, which the miserable man was unable to meet except by coming to England to earn it. It is still worse to know that the policy of extermination has so fully effected its object that the entire class has been swept from the soil, and the site of their holdings and homesteads is now becoming a profitless wilderness.

Letter XV

15th October, 1872

It would be extremely difficult to furnish even an approximate estimate of the number of Irish people resident in the agricultural districts of the four shires lying north of Lancashire and Yorkshire. From the mouth of the Tees to the Solway – from Morecambe Bay to Berwick – every town and considerable village has its Irish contigent of population. One can only judge of the total by the numbers known to reside in the chief agricultural towns and in the principal villages, and by inquiries generally from those well acquainted with the rural life of the North of England. From this rather indefinite basis of estimation it will be evident that any conclusions drawn must be merely conjectural and in such cases it is always safest and best to be under the mark. Omitting Carlisle, which has about a seventh of its population Irish – and the mining and iron districts of Northumberland and Durham, where large and flourishing Irish communities are found in every town, and almost in every village – the total number of Irish in the four Northern Counties of England may be safely put down at 6,000. In some of the less important towns they muster in considerable numbers. In still smaller places they are more or less numerous. In nearly every place where money can be earned either by toil or in petty traffic they are to be met with, cheerfully combatting the difficulties in their way, and, in many cases, in the end attaining to comfort and competence. Those who confine themselves to agricultural labour find here a better field for their exertions than in most other parts of England. The northern farmers pay higher wages than their class elsewhere, and in other respects, too, their labourers have superior advantages. Hence, the Irish labour-class who permanently settle in the smaller towns and villages, and find employment in the surrounding farmsteads, generally obtain good wages, and, if sober and frugal, can secure to themselves almost all that is necessary for their station in life.

But their numbers are comparatively few, and I can only give them a passing notice in estimating the grand total of the exiled children of Erin who have settled down in England. They, poor people, are the waifs scattered widest by the force which has broken and dispersed our race, yet in many respects they are infinitely better off than their kindred settled in the towns. But I cannot linger over their advantages or disadvantages, their toils and humble triumphs, their sorrows and their suffering. I can but note their existence, and pass on to where our people muster in thousands – strong in their energy, numbers, and intelligence, devoted in their patriotic attachment to their native land, and only awaiting the spell of unity to transform them into one of the most efficient forces in the labour necessary to work out her regeneration and redemption.

The population of Carlisle is in round numbers 30,000. Of these there are about 4,000 Irish. The calculation is made from the Catholic statistics of the town, with a due deduction for those not of Irish blood or birth. If this estimate be in error, it is not on the side of excess; but the influence of the Irish people here, whether socially or politically, is not proportionate to their numbers. Their political power is represented by rather under than over 500 votes, and their social state, except in few instances, is that of unskilled labourers and factory hands. Large numbers, particularly of the young, are employed in the cotton factories, the remainder in street labour or in the building trade. There are a few shopkeepers, and a larger number of hawkers and huxters, whose social condition is on a level with labour. But out of these social elements the Irish people in Carlisle have affected much for Religion and Education, and have provided amply for all their requirements in the future. There are two Catholic churches in the town sufficiently large for all present needs, and three schools affording accommodation for 600 children. In other respects, too, the condition of the Irish population of Carlise is satisfactory. The proportion of those who are fallen or indifferent is comparatively small. The one vice is drink; and its offspring, squalor and want, are observable in too many instances. But in Carlisle there is less evidence of the improvidence and vice which proceed from drink than in most of the other towns which I have visited.

From Carlisle to Newcastle, and the Irishman finds himself in the centre of a district in which he is surrounded by tens of thousands of his own kith and kin, many of whom have worked their way to competence, a few to independence, while the great bulk of them find constant employment at good wages, and are in a condition of comparative prosperity. It is, in truth, a high tribute to the industry and energy of the Irish people and furnishes the best and most conclusive rejoinder to the malicious libels of their slanderers, to find, wherever one turns here in England, whether in the haunts of toil or the centres of enterprise, their superior vigour and energy manifesting themselves in their struggles and in their success, and in every instance against adverse influences such as no other man in the community has had to encounter. Hard work and harsh treatment at first – then the usual advance due to skill, steadiness, and integrity – still the further advance after years of probation to the higher posts requiring care, judgment, and trained intelligence – these stages summarise the history of nearly every Irishman in England who as an employee has won for himself a leading position from his employers. Not alone does he owe nothing to favour, but his first step in the road to fair play must be in opposition to a host of prejudices, all of which he must encounter and overcome by the quiet but aggressive force of his innate good qualities. In Newcastle and district there are thousands of Irishmen who have thus won their way to positions regarded as high in the community of labour, while the great body of the people are found bearing the brunt of the severest toil, entirely heedless of its severity or drudgery so long as they can honestly win its rewards. The race reviled by Cockney scribblers proves itself, wherever it goes, the most laborious, industrious, and enduring. But a few years since, in an international test of strength, the highest example of physical power obtained by the *savants* who made the experiment was furnished by an Irish labourer in the London Docks, and he was but a type of his race. The men who work the hardest in England today, and who are most anxious for and constant at their work, are Irishmen. In the neighbourhood of Newcastle they are chiefly employed as labourers in the docks, on public works, in the mines, or in iron foundries – that is, in all works requiring the greatest strength, energy, and endurance – and in every instance they are found to be abreast or ahead of their competitors. In Newcastle, from a combination of causes, there are classes and varieties of labour to be obtained which are met with in few other places. It is the chief centre of the coal and iron trade of the North – a commercial port ranking among the highest in the scale of tonnage, and one of, it not the chief centre, of the English shipbuilding trade. In the multifarious employments belonging to each and all of these, Irish labourers, skilled and unskilled, are to be found; and in every instance – taking into consideration the short time they have been settlers in this locality and the difficulties which they have had to surmount – a fair proportion of their number have won for themselves foremost positions in the ranks of their fellow-workmen.

The population of Newcastle, according to the Census of 1871, is 130,000. Of them there are over 30,000 of Irish birth or Irish descent in the first generation, or about one in four of the total population – that is a proportion nearly equal to that prevailing in Manchester. But with this exceptionally large proportion of Irish to English in the town, their political influence, which ought to be great, is extremely limited. I have it on the written authority of leading Irishmen in the town who have the longest and best acquaintance with its political condition, and the best opportunity of arriving at a judgment of the political power possessed by the Irish element, that "there is no other town in England of the same Irish population where the Irish have less political weight than in Newcastle". This may be over scrupulous and severe self-judgment and condemnation, suggestive of hopeful contrition and resolution. Our friends in Newcastle have certainly the numbers that constitute power, and I saw evidence enough of the spirit and the ability necessary to make that power felt and respected. It is the same here as in many other places I have visited. The raw material of power is abundant. There is the highest patriotic spirit, and no lack of men capable of organising and directing the people. But there is a want of community in spirit – an absence of that sentiment which produces unity and the organisation which is absolutely essential to make the crude elements of political force a power to be exercised with effect. Why this is so in Newcastle is not for me to say. I merely record it, and suggest the remedy in so doing. I know there are Irishmen in the town with the spirit and will to combine and organise their fellow-countrymen in the service of Ireland. Where the spirit and the will exist, the way can hardly be wanting; and I have little doubt that a future record of the political condition of the Irish in Newcastle will show them united and prepared – forming among their kindred in England one of the most efficient aids in the pending struggle for the independence of their native land.

The social state of the 30,000 Irish in Newcastle will best be gauged by a reference to the employments in which they are engaged and the positions which they otherwise hold. In this respect they fairly contrast with their kindred in most other towns – indeed with all except Manchester and Liverpool. There are among them 400 business men of various grades and conditions, and over 4,000 skilled artisans, that is about 5,000 – or nearly one in six – who have worked upwards from the severest drudgery to a condition of comparative prosperity. There is still in the rank and file of labour, or dependent on it, 25,000. Of these there is a considerable number, particularly females, whose employment in factories and shops constitutes a species of skilled labour, but not of such a character as to raise those so engaged above the level of the ordinary labourer. In a community so constituted, and situated in the midst of a people where many are wealthy – the great bulk of the people in easy circumstances, and even those living by labour – in virtue of their being in previous possession – holding most of the best places – the social standing of the majority cannot lend much weight to their position. But if social position were to be meted by the higher standard of virtue and spiritual superiority, the contrast would be wholly in favour of the Irish. Dr. Todd's test of an angel from Heaven coming down to seek the best and purest, irrespective of social distinctions, would certainly find himself at home in more Irish than English houses in Newcastle.

There are four Catholic churches, including the Cathedral, in Newcastle, attended by nine priests and the Bishop. Schools sufficient to accommodate the Catholic children of the town are attached to these churches, in addition to which there is a superior school for some advanced pupils, and for children whose parents can afford them a higher class education. There are, besides these educational means, an Irish literary institute, with library and reading-room, where Irish literature stimulates and fosters national feeling, and the members meet for social communion or political consultation. The effect of all is that, for a community not otherwise too favourably situated for the promotion of morality, the moral condition of the Irish people stands high when contrasted with other towns. "A slight loss, owing to intemperance", summarises the statement furnished me regarding the male portion of the Irish people, whose state otherwise is reported as "fair" – while of the opposite sex it is said that they are "good", or rather would be, but for the evil influence of factories, workshops, and the immoral associates attaching to them. Of their bad effects "a slight falling off is the result". When there is much that is favourable I do not care to stop and inquire too minutely into the loss caused by intemperance, or the "slight falling off" due to still more pernicious influences. It is a sad and ungrateful task. Even in one instance it is a pleasure to say that I can accept a statement of the moral condition of our people without having to cloud its favourable aspect with the shadow of vice and ruin.

Across the Tyne stands the borough of Gateshead, the population of which, joined to The Felling, numbers 64,000. Of these, 20,000 – or a proportion nearly equal to that existing in Liverpool – are Irish. The borough, returns, if I rightly remember, two members to parliament. What, then is there to hinder the Irish people in this town from dictating the Irish politics of their members? Why should they not even return a member distinctively pledged to support the claims of Ireland? There can be little difficulty in doing this under the Ballot Act, which in England, so far as it has been tried, whether in municipal or parliamentary elections, has proved itself to be a voluntary disfranchising Act. It is the prevailing conviction in England that henceforth one-third of those possessing the franchise will decline to vote. This, of course, will give the Irish vote a relative preponderance, and enable the Irish population in nearly every town in England to dictate terms to the candidates. In such a place as Gateshead it will give them absolute power. This will be the more apparent when it is known that here a fair proportion of the population have attained to respectable positions, and should possess considerable influence. Judged by the standard of votes to population which I have found to prevail generally elsewhere, the Irish people of Gateshead should possess from 2,000 to 3,000 votes. Such political masses in a constituency no larger than this ought to be irresistible.

Hebburn and Garrow, standing six miles from Newcastle, contain 10,000 Irish in a population of 30,000; South Shields, eight miles from Newcastle, 5,000 Irish in 45,000; while in Walker, Wallsend, and Howden, five miles distant from Newcastle, is an Irish population of 10,000 in 23,000, being a larger proportion of Irish to English than I have found elsewhere, save in Wigan. The occupation, habits, and social condition of the people here are nearly the same as in Newcastle and Gatehead. The principal business in South Shields is shipping; Walker, Wallsend, and Howden, which may be regarded as one town, constitute the principal site of shipbuilding on the Tyne. There are two Catholic churches in Hebburn and Garrow, one in South Shields, and two in Walker, &c., with schools attached to each. In all other respects there is little difference in the condition of the Irish in Newcastle and these outlying districts, which, in truth, are but parts of a system of which Newcastle is the centre.

The same observation applies to North Shields, lying on the left or north side of the Tyne, and nine miles distant from Newcastle. Here the proportion of Irish to English is much smaller than in the places just mentioned, being only about 4,000 in 40,000, but the condition of the people is favourable socially, and morally even more favourable still. The churches and schools afford ample accommodation, and everything is fair and promising for the future; but as this town is not keeping pace with the other towns lying round Newcastle, and as a consequence will not attract to itself the energetic and the strong, it is not probable that here there will be much increase in the Irish population, or much change in their condition in the future.

There are engaged in the colliery districts lying within ten miles of Newcastle, an additional Irish population, numbering at a moderate computation 5,000 souls. Thus in the Vale of Tyne, and lying within a radius not exceeding ten miles, with Newcastle as the centre, there is an Irish population of 83,000, the great bulk of whom reside in and within a few miles of that town. Except in London, Liverpool, and Manchester, there is no such Irish force to be met with in England, and certainly none possessing in a higher degree the elements of present power and future success. There is no town in England where labour has more resolutely maintained its interests or more fully secured its rights, and none where the Irish labourer has more completely gained his recognised place in the ranks of his fellow workmen. The labouring population of Newcastle and the district have immense power at their command. Of this the Irish people have, or should have, their due share. In their own order, as well as among those who have risen out of their ranks, are many men of intelligence and ability well suited to organise and lead them. That they have the power no one can question who knows their numbers and estimates the influences they should possess by comparison with the surrounding English population. That they may use that power wisely and well – for the land that is dear to each one of them as to himself – is the sincere wish of one who is the friend and fellow-worker of all who counsel or act, think or toil, write or suffer for Ireland. Every Irishman owns allegiance to his native land, and no one should be exempt from a share in the labour which is the common duty of all.

Letter XVI

October 29, 1872

I have so far followed in the footsteps of our fellow-countrymen in England – indicated their fate and fortune, their struggles and their successes – pointed to the evidences of their faith and their charity, their zeal and their devotion – proclaimed to the world their patriotic spirit, their position, and their power, with the view of showing their available strength as a supplementary force in aid of the independence of their native land – shown the wreck and ruin that is everywhere the doleful complement of their hard-won prosperity, and proved to all who have traced with me the pathway of their progress, the superior power and endurance, spirit and energy, faith and virtue, of the race to which they belong. I have as fully and faithfully as circumstances permitted presented to your readers from week to week literal representations of Irish life in England. In so doing, I have visited the chief centres of Irish population in the towns and manufacturing districts, and have, as far as possible, verified by observation the statements received from those who had the best opportunity of knowing the true position and condition of our people. Though painted – as I admit they are – by the partial hand of friendship, the pictures I have drawn faithfully represent the life of the Irish people in England. Their failings and their vices, not less than their merits and their virtues, have been laid before the public. The evils of the system which has driven those who have fallen from health and happiness, purity and virtue, in their own land, to disease and misery, vice and crime, in the towns of England, I have pointed to and denounced, in the hope of arousing to more earnest exertion the patriot and the priest, the philanthropist and social reformer, to arrest the causes at home whose effects are here visible in the destruction of the souls and bodies of the thousands – nay, the tens, the hundreds of thousands of poor victims who have been, and are daily, thrust into the thoroughfares of vice, to be hurried on in the foul crush to the precipice of ruin over which they pass, and whence there is no return. Every condition and phase of Irish life in England I have portrayed – every virtue noted – every element of strength calculated – every source of evil laid bare. A few general observations on the total strength, present power, and future prospects of our brethren in England will appropriately close a correspondence which I venture to hope has not been barren of good results both to the Irish in England and their brethren at home.

The total number of Irish resident in England can only be estimated approximately, but the elements of approximation are at hand, and the deductions drawn from them self-evident. There are in England and Wales considerably over a million, probably a million and a quarter, of the population of Irish birth. There is at the *very lowest* computation an equal number who are children of Irish parents born in England, and who in everything but in the accident of being born out of Ireland are as Irish are their parents. This would give a total Irish population of at least 2,500,000, or over one in ten of the entire population, which, according to the recent census, numbers 22,704,108 souls. This estimate of the Irish population in England corresponds in a general way with the total of the approximate population which I have derived from a computation of the Irish population in the towns and districts which I have visited, or of which I have received special information. But there is still another and independent means of computation, which in a general manner corroborates the preceding approximations. The excess of increase of population in England in the two last decennial periods – that is, from 1861 to 1871, over and above natural increase, must be credited to immigration. This excess was in the main due to Irish immigration, and the figures which represent it may almost be taken to represent an increase of the Irish population in England. This increase, with a calculation in the same ratio extending back to 1845 – and without including in the calculation the Irish resident in England previous to that date – would make a total of over a million souls, so that all available methods of computation point to nearly the same result. The supplementary census tables, which, if issued, I have not been able to obtain, may furnish accurate information of the nationality of the people resident in England on the 3rd of April 1872. I have little doubt that, should they do so, it will be found that a total of *born* Irish residents in England, which I here give, will but very little vary from the number furnished by the official statistics – and this being so, my estimate of the total number of Irish, either by blood or birth, at present domiciled in England cannot fall short of the estimate I here furnish. In London alone the Irish population is little short of 500,000. The Archbishop of Westminster recently declared that there were in London and district 200,000 Irish Catholics known to the priests. I am afraid that nearly as many more are resident there of whom the priests have but imperfect knowledge. Indeed, a note received today through a friend in London informs me from an official source that there is no proper Catholic census of London in existence, and the same may be said of all or nearly all the larger towns. But taking every element of calculation into the account, and including the Irish population of all denominations, the number of our race resident in London cannot be much under half a million. If to this number we add the Irish population of Manchester, Liverpool, and one or two other large towns, our estimate will reach a million souls – and it will be at once evident that I am not over the mark in stating that south of the Tweed there resides an Irish population of two millions and a half.

A brief consideration of the present condition and future fate of this large and rapidly advancing portion of our kindred cannot fail to be interesting to all who have at heart the power and prosperity of the scattered Irish people, and who hold that, however dispersed and wherever resident, the Celtic race is one and indivisible – that, in the words of the poet,

> One in name and in fame are the sea-divided Gaels

I have pointed out their power, position, and influence, locally and shall here, therefore, confine myself to a consideration of their condition as a whole, as a foreign and peculiar element resident among a people different in habits, tastes, religion, and sentiment, and to whose absorbing influences they have nothing to oppose but the inflexible individuality which has marked their race from its first appearance in the dawn of European history and which has preserved their native land a nation through seven centuries of foreign domination, in which every agent to destroy national sentiment and degrade the people mentally and morally to the level of tame and timid provincialism has been tried, and tried in vain. The Irish race has absorbed many races and never been absorbed by any – has been repeatedly overcome, but never conquered; but never before – and, indeed, in no place now but in England – has it been placed in such a trying position to test the invincibility of its resistance, the energy of its self-sustension and power of expansion – at the same time assimilating to itself all with which it comes in contact. At home it had but to concentrate itself and oppose its energy to external force. Here there are elements of opposition in creed as well as in nationality which assail the Irishman at every turn and test his fidelity to the utmost, while – more sinister still – are the various social agencies which both in his hours of labour and relaxation insidiously surround his daily life and gradually insinuate themselves into his thoughts and his habits, with no counteracting influence but those derived from limited association with his compatriots, and the inspiration which he draws from the public life and literature of his native land. This, it will be seen, is a trying test of fidelity and endurance, and the wisest and most thoughtful of the Irishmen resident in England begin to ask themselves: How long will their creed and national sentiment preserve them as a distinct and separate people – a nation within a nation? This position of the Irish in England, and the probable results arising therefrom, may be thus succinctly put – indeed, it has been put to me so often and so earnestly that I think it necessary to refer to it here. The source from which Irish immigration to England proceeded is practically exhausted – that is, emigration from Ireland to England has almost ceased, and henceforth there will be no supply to strengthen and bear new life into the Irish communities in the English towns. The result will be a partial isolation, with a gradual increase in the effect of surrounding English influences.

Then there are three causes at work which are gradually sapping the strength of the Irish communities. There is, first, a large drain on their strength by emigration to America and the colonies. This was particularly so during the "cotton famine", when the Irish population in the towns of Lancashire decreased by thousands. The Irish population in Wigan alone during that period showed a decrease of 2,000. Constant work and good wages have, since that time, arrested this wholesale drain, but there is a constant and exhaustive decline due to this cause alone. Then there are two other active and vicious causes of decay always in operation, which must, in the end, if not checked, lead to an excessive decline of the strength of the Irish in the English towns. These causes are at work at the extremes of Irish society. At the top there is a class – fortunately not large in numbers, but not less baleful in their example and its results – who, having attained to comparative prosperity, wish to forget their nativity, and in all things conform to English thought and English habit. They commence by simulating everything English, and end by being what they seem. Their defection is greatly facilitated by intermarriage with English families, and the consequent conformity which follows. The loss, numerically, could be borne; but the misfortune is, that the class which feeds this defection is the class whose means would enable them to be of the greatest benefit to their country and their kindred did they not thus fall away from the standard of patriotic duty. The genus "flunkey" is not so common here as at home, but it is unfortunately common enough in this class to be productive of most pernicious results.

But it is from the other end of the social scale that the Irish in England sustain the severest and saddest loss. I have repeatedly, in the course of this correspondence, referred to the dreadful losses entailed on the Irish by the vice and crime consequent on their associations in the English towns, and the general demoralising influence of all their surroundings, and have often turned saddened and sickened from its contemplation, and passed silently over what would otherwise furnish but a monotonous diorama of vice and decay. The picture painted of one town might be taken generally to apply to all, and it was only necessary to know the population to estimate the percentage of loss. Here, then is a drain on the vital power and force of the people which I cannot accurately calculate, and can only say that it is enormous. At the very least – and making all allowances for those who are but errant in evil and of whom reform may be expected – the Irish people in England sacrifice a tithe of their numbers to the dread demons that infest the society in which their circumstances compel them to live. There is certainly no exaggeration in this, but the contrary; so that from the good, the pure, the pious body of the Irish people in England, there is this dreadful decrease to be struck off before we can enter into any calculation of the power of resisting the other influences which tend to their absorption in, and asssimlation with, the social elements of English life.

There is, I am satisfied, a constant decrease of an eighth of the Irish population in England from all those causes; and hence it is contended that as this proportion is nearly equal to the natural increase of the people, it is only a question of time till the entire Irish element is drawn into the life of the English people.

The conclusion arrived at from these considerations is that the Irish in England have but to accept the decree of destiny and submit to their fate. Such a conclusion I have heard expressed more than once – have had to decry it whenever I heard it – and think it necessary to do so now. The dangers are more apparent than real, and the circumstances of the future are such as to lessen, if not prevent, many of the evils which in the past have destroyed the people, and which still leaves behind them the traces of their ruin. Much of what is evil in the Irishman's lot is due to association, but much more to ignorance and want of the spiritual supervision and direction which in the first period of the exodus it was found impossible to supply, and which even yet is supplied but imperfectly. Gradually the social condition of the whole body of the Irish in England is being raised, and with the means will come education and enlightenment. Indeed, the means of education *must* be provided, and may now be said to be at every poor man's door. Fewer of the young will fall into the sink of crime, and elevation of tone, sentiment, and morals will be the natural growth of increased intelligence. But precisely as that intelligence is in harmony with the faith and national sentiment of Ireland, will be the safety and salvation of the Irish in England. It is only one step from conformity with English ways to conformity with English morals and English indifference, and he who attempts to discover the associations which bind the Irish people to their native land commits a crime, the consequences of which would prove as ruinous to faith as to the morals of the people. Everything good which the Irish in England have preserved is their own; their vices in nine cases out of ten are acquired. A closer conformity to English life would destroy the former and extend the latter. Close and constant union with Ireland in all things is their safety and security. While their inspiration and their hopes are drawn from the sacred soil of their birth, while they regard themselves as but a section of the race whose source and centre is in Ireland, while they resist change and defy the absorbing influence of race – in a word, while the Irishmen in England are true to Faith and Fatherland, there is no power in England, whether political or social, that can divert their destiny or check their progress. To live in isolation is impossible. The duties of citizenship, the necessities of existence, preclude the possibility of living in a state which would be no better than sordid selfishness. In social and religious affairs it is safe to be among but not of the English people. In matters of daily life, whether relating to progress or politics, it is the right and the duty of the Irish people in England to assert and maintain their rights – to use their power and influence for the benefit of their native land – to seize every occasion of making that power felt, and resist every effort to limit or control it – and as the sole and certain means of accomplishing all which they desire to cultivate harmony and union, not only locally, but through the entire body of their race in England. It would not be difficult to organise the whole of the Irish power in England, so that movement at any one point would vibrate through the entire body and summon them all to united action at the call of duty. The means to accomplish this are in the hands of the people. The evils which alone could mar it are party spirit and abuse of power for personal and selfish aims.

But there is little fear of this. The great body of the Irish in England are true and zealous, patriotic and pure, constant in their fatih, unchanging in their patriotic devotion to their native land. Their industry has made them prosperous; and though the multitude are still in the ranks of labour, their influence is a potent element in public life – their force a power in the land which must be respected. Indeed, it is not too much to say that, in virtue of their power, if wisely exercised, they have to a very great extent the future of their native land in their guardianship. They have become so powerful as to be in a position to force their opinions on the people of England, who but a few years since regarded their claims with contemptuous indifference. They are now sought where they were heretofore repelled, their opinions solicited, and their judgment respected. There are still impediments in their way, but nothing but what is trivial and will yield to earnest resolution and persistent efforts. To make themselves felt and respected socially and naturally, the one thing needed is close and compact organisation – the thing to be avoided is being drawn in the tail of English parties, or being used for purely English purposes. Mutual interchange of service with the English people, is, of course, distinct from this, and may be adopted with advantage to both sides. But as the great cardinal aim of the Irish people at home and abroad is to secure for the cradle of our race – the home of our memories and affections, the inestimable boon of national independence, every other aim and object should be subordinated to this. This is the labour of the hour. To effect it the "wisest and best" in the land have devoted heart and brain, soul and spirit, and, beside them, the Irish in England have taken their stand with a zeal and earnestness which show that in the coming struggle they are ready to take their place and do their duty. With all the faults and the losses which we contemplate with pain, there is the grandeur and the greatness which ever distinguished the race from which they spring. They are sullied by the associations with which they are surrounded, but have retained through all the virtues derived from their ancestors. They have passed through the ordeal of tribulation and mourning, and now behold the hope and promise of the future. That hope is to see their native land crowned with the glory and the light of freedom. The desire which is dearest to their hearts is to share in the struggle for her liberties, and write their names on the roll of those whose fame shall go down to all posterity as her deliverers. The faith which has preserved our land a nation through 700 years, and which stirs the heart of her children over the earth today, has nowhere a holier shrine or more endearing sanctuary than in the faithful and patriotic bosoms of the Irish in England.

Notes to Text

*I wish to express my thanks to Michael Hurst and Sheridan Gilley for their vital assistance in compiling the notes.

[1] John Henry Foley and Patrick MacDowell. The former was responsible for Asia and the latter for Europe.

[2] Justin McCarthy, for example, was at the forefront of London journalism.

[3] W.G. Todd, "The Irish in England", *Dublin Review*, lxxxii (December 1856), pp.470-521; reprinted with additions, *The Irish in England* (London 1857).

[4] Henry Mayhew, *The Great World of London* (London 1856).

[5] Henry Edward Manning (subsequently cardinal).

[6] Alexander Pope, Essay on Man, Esp. 2, lines 217-18. Heinrick misquoted Pope slightly and the passage should have read:

> Monster of so such frightful mien,
> to be hated, needs but be seen

[7] *The Tempest*, Act II, 2, line 42. Heinrick's version is slightly inaccurate and should read "misery acquaints a man with strange bedfellows".

[8] The mission was founded in 1831. For its history see, Bernard W. Kelly, *Historical Notes on English Catholic Missions* (London 1907), p.235.

[9] John A. Roebuck, born 1801, died 1879, a well-known radical M.P. (Bath 1832-37; 1841-47; Sheffield 1849-69; 1874-79).

[10] Lord Hartington was then Chief Secretary for Ireland in the Liberal Cabinet; William Keogh had been a member of the Independent Irish party in the 1850s who accepted an Irish judgeship and in 1872 rendered an infamous (in nationalist circles) decision on the Galway by-election which made particular note of clerical intimidation.

[11] Philip Casey, Assistant Secretary, South Yorkshire Miners' Association.

[12] The Preston by-election on 26 September 1872 returned the Conservative with a majority of 718. Although the Irish wished to make some claim to influencing the result, the Conservative majority was reduced from the general election of 1868. At the general election of 1874 both Conservative candidates were returned by larger majorities than in 1872.

[13] Thomas Moore "Paradise and the Speri", lines 205-6. The lines should read:

> Some flow'rets of Eden ye still inherit,
> But the trail of the serpent is over them all.

[14] Robert Lowe, minister in the Liberal Government.

[15] Thomas Davis, "A Song for the Irish Militia". See T.W. Rolleston, introduction, *Thomas Davis: Selections from his Prose and Poetry* (Dublin n.d.), p.352.

[16] Reference to irregular Turkish troops responsible for the massacre of the Bulgars.

[17] Refers to those who evicted Irish tenants.

Index